# VISIO
# DIVINA

"Jesus said to her, 'Everyone who drinks of this water will be thirsty again, but those who drink of the water that I will give them will never be thirsty. The water that I will give will become in them a spring of water gushing up to eternal life.'" JOHN 4:13–14 NRSV

# VISIO DIVINA

*A New Prayer Practice
for Encounters with God*

## KAREN KUCHAN

*A Crossroad Book*
The Crossroad Publishing Company
New York

The Crossroad Publishing Company
16 Penn Plaza – 481 Eighth Avenue, Suite 1550
New York, NY 10001

Scripture quotations are from the New Revised Standard Version Bible,
copyright © 1989 by the Division of Christian Education of the National Council of the Churches of Christ in the U.S.A., or from The
Holy Bible: New International Version, copyright © 1973, 1978, 1984
by International Bible Society. All Rights Reserved.

The text is set in 11.5/16 Kochin and 10.5/16 Goudy Sans.
The display fonts are Charlemagne, Nuptial Script, and Vintage.

Printed in the United States of America

**Library of Congress Cataloging-in-Publication Data**
Kuchan, Karen.
    Visio divina : a new prayer practice for encounters with God /
Karen Kuchan.
        p.   cm.
    Includes bibliographical references and index.
    ISBN 0-8245-2317-2 (alk. paper)
    1. Prayer – Biblical teaching.  2. Spiritual life – Christianity.
    3. Rest – Religious aspects – Christianity.  4. Grace (Theology)
    I. Title.
BS680.P64K83 2005
248.3′2 – dc22

                                                          2005025671

1   2   3   4   5   6   7   8   9   10            10   09   08   07   06   05

*To my friend Catherine,*
*who didn't experience all that Love could transform*
*and all that Life had to offer*

# CONTENTS

## FAITH
## EXPERIENCING GOD
## 31

## HOPE
### THE OPPOSITE OF HOPELESSNESS
### 91

## LOVE
### BEING LOVED AND LOVING OTHERS
### 117

# Vɪ/ɪo Dɪvɪnᴀ

*What is it?*

Knowing God through Visio Divina radically changed my experience of life, my understanding of God, and my ability to love myself and others. In my work as a spiritual director I'm seeing God change the lives of others through Visio Divina. What is it? How does it work? How can I experience it? These are a few of the questions I asked when I was first introduced to the concept of transformation of the soul through prayer.

Visio Divina is a Latin term which means "divine seeing." Recalling the sixth-century Benedictine practice of Bible reading called lectio divina in which one meditates on a passage of scripture allowing the Spirit to speak through the story, Visio Divina is a prayer practice that facilitates a revelation of God through the opened eyes of one's heart. The term Visio Divina came to me a few years ago while writing my PhD dissertation as a way to describe a prayer practice that integrates two models of prayer: traditional contemplative prayer and a form of prayer that facilitates experiencing God's presence through the charisms of grace. "Charism" is a Greek word that describes the movement of the Spirit through a person or community in a way that reveals God's presence. "Charisms of grace," therefore, are ways the Spirit moves through an individual or community, mediating God's grace to others. "Gifts of the Spirit" is another way of describing the same movement of the Spirit. Catholics usually use the term "charisms of grace" and Protestants often use the term "gifts of the Spirit." By allowing God's presence to be mediated through these charisms/gifts, Visio Divina is a unique prayer practice with its roots both in the richness of the Catholic contemplative tradition and a biblically based understanding (1 Corinthians 12, Ephesians 4) of the role of the Spirit as mediated by the charisms of grace that facilitate healing of the soul. This integration of a contemplative prayer practice with an understanding of the mediation of grace through the body of Christ introduces us in Visio Divina to a new way of praying, one that creates in us space to be encountered by God, enabling us to know God better and experience God's love more fully.

Contemplative prayer is a type of prayer that encourages sinking into God's presence within ourselves. Two forms of Christian mysticism contribute to our knowledge of contemplative prayer. Apophatic mysticism emphasizes a way of knowing God absent of images, symbols, and words. The focus of apophatic mysticism is on the nature of God that is beyond image, symbol, or word, yet can be known through contemplative prayer. Affective mysticism, on the other hand, focuses on an experience of God that incorporates images, symbols, and words. The affective tradition helps us understand spiritual experiences that can be felt with our senses, such as sight, sound, and touch. In both versions of contemplative prayer, God is experienced within the soul.

As we sink into God's presence within, emotions and thoughts come to the surface and reveal places within our soul that long for integration and wholeness. This longing for integration and wholeness describes a path toward finding God within and experiencing healing of the places within our soul that have been hurt or neglected and are longing to be restored. During contemplative prayer God's presence within facilitates the release of emotions that need to be grieved which originate in those past painful experiences of hurt and neglect. As we feel the emotions that are rooted in the past painful experiences we've endured, we begin to experience ourselves in ways less influenced by those experiences. The practice of contemplative prayer over time enables us to connect to our soul so that emotions that interfere with experiencing union with God can be released. The release of these emotions helps us experience God's presence within and helps us in the process of becoming the person God created us to be.

However, in Visio Divina we combine this kind of contemplative prayer with an additional element — an experience of God mediated through charisms of grace so that a new form of prayer emerges where we experience both God's presence within and God's mediated presence bringing healing to our soul. According to scripture, the charisms of grace that mediate God's presence of healing include words of knowledge, words of wisdom, discernment, prophecy, mercy, and healing. All of these charisms are ways God reveals God's self to offer encouragement, hope, and healing. The apostle Paul describes the gifts this way.

> *Now to each one the manifestation of the Spirit is given for the common good. To one there is given through the Spirit the message of wisdom, to another the message of knowledge by means of the same Spirit, to another faith by the same Spirit, to another gifts of healing by that one Spirit, to another miraculous powers, to another prophecy, to another*

*distinguishing between spirits.... All these are the work of*
*one and the same Spirit, and he gives them to each one, just*
*as he determines.*                    — 1 Corinthians 12:7–11

Visio Divina is a prayer practice that facilitates an experience of God that offers hope and encouragement while healing the soul and can be facilitated by spiritual directors, pastoral counselors, soul friends, and others in the helping professions. As a spiritual director, I facilitate Visio Divina with my directees in a private practice setting. Visio Divina is one expression of spiritual direction that can be integrated with other practices and ways of being present with a person while providing soul care and spiritual guidance. Though best facilitated in pairs, it can be experienced individually as one learns how to engage in this contemplative prayer practice on one's own. I hope you, the reader, find this book helpful as you learn to engage in this prayer practice.

When God encounters us during Visio Divina, God begins to reveal unconscious places within our soul that need to be understood, felt, and healed. As the unconscious motives of our heart are revealed, we begin to understand ourselves better, why we do what we do and feel what we feel. As a result, we learn the sources of our ongoing struggles with behaviors we cannot change

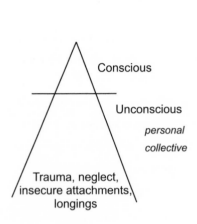

and why we have a hard time loving and receiving love from God and others. Sometimes we cannot change our behavior, because that behavior is rooted in deep unconscious places of hurt and neglect. Until the source of the hurt and neglect is healed, it is hard to change the behavior. In Visio Divina God reveals those places of hurt and neglect and enables us to know God's presence at the places where those experiences shape our behavior and limit our ability to love and be loved.

During Visio Divina, as we enter into a place of rest and experience God's presence revealing the motives of

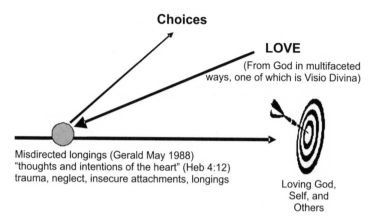

our heart, the Spirit reveals Jesus through the opened eyes of our heart. Hebrews 4:12 helps me understand this reality. This passage of scripture speaks of the word of God being alive and active like a double-edged sword dividing soul from spirit, revealing the motives of our heart. When we enter into God's rest (Hebrews 4:1–3), the word of God is Jesus the Logos (John 1:1) who is alive and active penetrating our heart, revealing what needs to be known so we can understand why we do what we do. One way of understanding this passage is to think about "rest" as participating in the completed cosmic work of God. Judith Wray, a New Testament scholar, suggests we do that. Rest, therefore, can be a place of participating in what God has already accomplished on our behalf — the death and resurrection of

Christ. Our participation in his death and resurrection enables us to experience the love, grace, and freedom this event accomplished.

The way the author of Ephesians prays for the church at Ephesus as presented in Ephesians 1:18 is another illustration of Visio Divina. The prayer is that the eyes of our heart be enlightened as we come to know God. The word "heart" in the Bible means not just emotions but also our mind, will and our emotions. So, the desire is that all of our soul — the mind, will, and emotions — would be opened as we come to know God. Indeed, recent researchers in the area of psychobiology confirm this fuller understanding of the "heart" as the seat of the soul by telling us that our brain as an organ of consciousness consists of two hemispheres; a left side responsible for analytical thought and a right side responsible for emotions, imagination, and sense experience (sight, smell, taste, touch, and sound). In other words, when Paul prays that the "eyes of our heart" be enlightened, he is praying that we would know God through all our consciousness, our analytical mind as well as through our emotions, imagination, and senses.

In Visio Divina, the eyes of our heart are enlightened, and the Spirit brings wisdom and revelation as to who God is. The Spirit of wisdom and revelation connects with us in such a way that our emotions, imagination, and senses are encountered by God. We then reflect on this experience and begin to understand it by using the analytical left side of our brain. During Visio Divina God first connects with us through our imagination, emotions and senses and then the more rational side of our brain begins to understand it. As a result, we begin to know in a way that connects our head knowledge about God with our heart knowledge of God. In this way, Visio Divina helps integrate our head with our heart.

So, who is the God who encounters us this way? God is relational. Visio Divina is about a relationship. It's a relationship based on trust — like any good relationship. It is easier to trust a person you know, and Visio Divina helps us get to know the God we are invited to trust.

I got to know this God much better while I attended a school for spiritual directors at a Benedictine monastery in Pecos, New Mexico. Although my journey of transformation through Visio Divina began years before, experiences of healing continued in Pecos as God brought new insight into my soul's longing for integration and wholeness. These experiences of insight and healing significantly contributed to my ability to communicate about Visio Divina, and I doubt whether you would be reading the book in your hands if I hadn't cooperated with God in the transformation of my soul. I share this experience in hopes that you, the reader, will catch a glimpse of just how important Visio Divina has been in my life.

On my first day of a month of being immersed in the movements of monastic life, Karen, my spiritual director, suggests I listen to my dreams as a way to learn about my soul. I agree without much expectancy that my soul will do much talking, as it had never spoken up very loudly through dreams in the past. The quiet, meditative mountain monastery that became my spiritual home was conducive to inviting the inner voice of my soul to make images that would eventually enable God to bring healing to one of my heart's deepest fears.

As I lie in bed in my simple, rustic room I am vaguely aware of images in my conscious awareness, and I light my candle, grab a pen, and open my journal to record what my soul wants me to know.

I see myself talking on the phone with the men's basketball coach of my high school alma mater. I tell him that I'm calling to show support for his team because when I was a player in high school, the men never supported the women's team, even though we always won league championships. I say to this men's basketball coach that I'd like to meet him. The next scene that my soul creates is my interacting with this coach who I learn is also a postmodern impressionist painter and is very attractive to me. The dance begins. He asks me what I do for a living. I begin to tell him about Visio Divina and my work as a spiritual director in private practice. He seems to be getting frustrated and takes me into a science lab at the school and points to an anatomy skeleton that hangs from the wall. I know he is inviting me to explain Visio Divina by using this scientific, concrete and analytic way of knowing. I can't do it. How do I explain the transformation of the soul in a lab designed to study the concrete parts of the physical body? The soul can't be studied that way. Modernity inspired rational, scientific, and factual knowledge. No wonder we don't understand very well the way of the cross in transforming the soul. I can't explain it in an anatomy lab, so I walk outside, feeling rejected by the man who wants to understand me. He walks over to the gym to lift weights, which reinforces his need for strength and power. As I cry while sitting on the curb, he walks out of the gym, pulls out two guns and begins to shoot at me. I frantically get up and run down the streets of Pasadena, the home of my office where I work with clients each week. I am running in a white robe that I wear when I rest and experience renewal through massage therapy. My white robe can't hold my guns and I drop them as I run away from this man who says, "In order to ascend in my faith, I must kill a woman. I've chosen you to be the one I'll kill." The race continues and I finally find safety in a white car, similar to the 1980 MG I purchased a few years ago. I feel safe in my car and drive away, escaping the threat of being shot down by this man in my dream.

I meet with Karen and ask, "So, what in the heck does that mean?" We begin to process the symbolism and meanings of the people in my dream. I learn that my soul is communicating a desire for integration between the masculine and feminine parts of my being. I learn that I fear being shot down by my own inner masculine who has been trained in analytical thinking and scientific reasoning (my undergraduate degree was in biology). He wants to shoot me down because I am a woman who can't explain Visio Divina in a way that his highly rational and concrete mind can understand. In order for the man to ascend in his faith, he must shoot down the feminine voice because it is the masculine mind of rationality that has been valued in the place where I am being asked to teach and write. Prior to becoming a sojourner to my new spiritual home in New Mexico, I was asked to teach a course in a seminary that highly values the rational at the expense of the feminine intuitive and creative voice. My dream reveals that my little girl desires to be integrated with her inner masculine in such a way that the feminine voice of knowledge and wisdom can freely speak of her journey of healing and likewise encourage and teach others to embrace their own journey of integration and transformation.

The next day, during one of our quiet meditations, I sense an image coming into my conscious awareness. It's a little girl in a pretty dress sitting on her bed in her room alone. She seems sad. I feel her sadness and a tightness in my chest. Then, Jesus walks into the room and sits beside her, puts his arm around her and begins to lead her to the hallway where a little boy is waiting for them. He's wearing basketball shoes and a baseball hat. The little girl is timid and shy, not sure if the little boy will want to play with her. Jesus puts his arm around the little boy while he has his other arm around the little girl; all three of them walk down the hallway and out the door to a playground. Jesus invites us to play together. The little girl is still afraid...and I still feel the tightness in my chest, but because the little girl has experienced Jesus so many times before, she trusts him, and agrees to venture off with little boy. They first do an art project together, then push each other on a swing and then play catch with a baseball. I realize my chest doesn't feel tight anymore and begin to feel the joy of playing with this little boy. I like him and he likes me.

A few weeks later, after more experiences of integration and healing, another image comes into my mind during a quiet meditation. I'm a grown woman wearing a white dress and basketball shoes! I'm teaching a group of people about Visio Divina. I feel good, and the image communicates the integration that has occurred within my soul. Day 28 of my spiritual pilgrimage among my new friends of Catholics, Protestants, monks, and sisters. I'm invited to write a poem that shares my journey of integration while being trained as a spiritual director among the saints. I reflect on my experiences of healing and my soul's communication through numerous dreams. I pick up the pen to write about a dance with God that began many years ago and still continues today.

This poem traces the path of one aspect of healing I've experienced during this past month. Day 2 of our twenty-eight-day adventure brought to the surface a fear of failure that I was unaware of struggling with. You see, in the past six months I've been working with an editor on a book on prayer and healing and a few weeks before coming to our school I was invited to teach a class at a seminary. Although I felt honored that an editor wanted to publish my work and the seminary wanted me to teach, I became aware that I write, teach, and lead from a feminine side that has been abused by a masculine-oriented system of higher education and neglected by my father. As I continued to experience God's healing presence here at the monastery, I realized that my fear of failure was a fear that the feminine would be rejected — not by the masculine environment that I feared, but by my own inner masculine that was not yet one with my feminine. This poem comes from my feminine voice.

*Dancing in White*
*I came....*
*afraid that I would never be heard*
*by the men who need to hear my voice.*
*The man who was trying to shoot me down*
*showed up in a dream and I learned it was myself.*
*I didn't like that man because he didn't like me.*
*I am a little girl dressed in pink.*
*He's a little boy wearing a baseball cap.*
*Jesus said he wanted to love me.*
*I got excited... could it be true?*
*Could the man in the dream really want to love me?*
*I'm tired of running from him*

*I am tired of not being heard*
*I want him to love me.*

*Jesus brought us together*
*We played on a swing*
*he was fun . . .*
*he takes risks . . .*
*likes to do flips . . .*
*and is good at baseball . . .*
*I like flowers . . .*
*Wearing pink dresses . . .*
*and dancing with Jesus. . . .*

*I'm all grown up now.*
*I'm ready to teach and to write*
*I'm ready to guide men and women*
*in the ministry of spiritual direction*
*A ministry to see lives transformed*
*by the power of the cross*
*and the presence of Christ*
*Who loves little children*
*And longs to set them free.*

*I wear white dresses*
*And I dance with Jesus*
*I love the mind he has given me*

*I want to use it to serve others*
*who don't yet dance with Jesus*
*and who don't yet know*
*the love who is integrating my soul.*

This Love who is integrating my soul continues the process which will not be completed until I am in union with God for eternity. Since my experience at the Benedictine monastery, God continues to take me to places within my soul that long for integration and wholeness. In the following pages I'll share more of my story as well as the stories of others who have experienced the Source of love and are being transformed as they are encountered by grace. Visio Divina changed my life. I'd like to try to introduce it in hope that it might do the same for you.

In summary, Visio Divina integrates two forms of Christian prayer. The contemplative nature of Visio Divina encourages us to sink into God's presence within, allowing thoughts and emotions to be released which interfere with experiencing union with God. Charisms of grace mediate God's presence of healing and facilitate an experience of God that brings healing to the soul. The practice of Visio Divina can be understood as entering into God's rest where Jesus, the Logos, is living and active, penetrating the soul and revealing the motives

of the heart. The unconscious sources of hurt and neglect are revealed which contribute to behavior we can't
change and our struggles with loving and being loved by
God and others. God encounters us through the opened
eyes of our heart, and we experience God in our emotions, imagination, and senses in the places of neglect and
hurt within our soul. The experience of God through the
opened eyes of our heart contributes to knowing God
better, experiencing love, and hoping in the experiential
reality of God's love that we can actually feel. Therefore,
Visio Divina helps us experience faith, hope, and love.

### *Journaling*
#### *A companion as you travel your path*

*Journaling can be a helpful way for you to keep a record of your
thoughts and feelings while you read this book and begin to experience Visio Divina on your own. Begin by finding something
to write on that you feel comfortable with. Some people like a
big book with pages they can fill with pictures, drawings, photos
and words. Others like smaller books with lined pages so they
can write their thoughts in a more structured way. It's not important to have a specific kind of journal; what's important is*

*that you feel comfortable with it. It's yours. Choose something that reflects you.*

*Here is a simple way you can record your thoughts and feelings as you journal. Remember, this is only a sample. If another way feels more comfortable for you, do it that way.*

*Record what you feel about a given experience in Visio Divina and then record what you think about that experience. It's helpful to journal both your feelings and thoughts as your reflect on these experiences. You can write down the experience of Visio Divina and then write on separate pages the questions How do I feel? What do I think?*

*Remember, what's important is for you to feel comfortable with your journal and to use it as a place for ongoing dialogue with God and your self regarding your experiences as you read this book and begin to be encountered by God through Visio Divina.*

You'll find three sections in this book, entitled Faith, Hope, and Love. These are called the theological virtues by the Catholic Church and are central to spiritual formation and growth by all those who profess faith in God. Visio Divina can contribute to a person's deepening relationship with God and, therefore, spiritual growth in these three areas. Each section of the book contains chapters centered on one specific aspect of faith, hope, and love. 1 Corinthians 13 reminds us about faith, hope, and love and highlights that the greatest of these is love. The purpose of this book is to introduce you to a way of being loved by God that can help you love your self better so that, in turn, you can share that love with others.

# FAITH

## EXPERIENCING GOD

Do I have to change in order to be accepted by God? Can I expect God to love me in a tangible way? How do I learn how to be open to love? How can I get to know the God I'm supposed to trust? How can I learn to trust if I've been abandoned? Will God be with me in my mess? I address these questions in the following section as I share stories of people who experienced God through Visio Divina.

Spiritual formation is the way God forms you into who you were created to be and into God's likeness. Visio Divina is crucial to your spiritual formation because the primary purpose for Visio Divina is for you to come to experience and therefore know God better. As you know

God better, you can more easily learn to love as God loves. We love because Christ first loved us (1 John 4:19). Visio Divina enables you to experience Christ loving you in practical and tangible ways, and as Christ loves you, you'll know better how to love others. As the eyes of your heart are opened, the Word of God, Jesus, begins to reveal how past hurts and painful experiences have shaped you. As God begins to love you in those past experiences, they will have less influence on your present choices and behavior. The greatest commandment is to love God and to love our neighbor as we love ourselves. Visio Divina can help us do this better.

# ONE

# ACCEPTANCE

*Do I have to change in order to be
accepted by God?*

I had been a Christian most of my life. Sure, I wan-
dered away from the faith for most of my high school
and college years as my journey led me to lots of different
places in my search to experience love and acceptance.
My deep longing to be loved was expressed in many different forms, one of which was being very, very driven
to accomplish goals and perform as a successful college
basketball player and pre-med student. Every once in a
while I felt I had earned my way to being loved when
I scored enough points to feel good about myself or got
an "A" on a biology exam. But most of the time I didn't
feel loved. In my attempt to feel the emotions of being
loved, such as comfort, security, and acceptance, I chose
an addictive relationship with food that never satisfied the
deepest longings of my soul. Although I was a Christian,

the deep longings of my soul went unfulfilled, resulting in behavior I couldn't change and an ongoing struggle with not feeling loved and feeling limited in my ability to love others.

A few years later, I moved to Flagstaff, Arizona, where I was on staff with a ministry working with high school and college students. While in Flagstaff, I learned a lot about Christianity and a God who desired to heal and give hope to hurting people. I didn't know I was hurting then. I was too busy leading a successful ministry, serving others and building my kingdom, oh...guess it's God's kingdom...to be hurting. There was too much to do, too many lives to be saved, too many hurting people to help, too many books to be read, too many awards to be earned, and too many people to please. I'm thankful that my mentor, Duane, introduced me to the concept of abiding with God. I began to learn how to hang out with God while spending time with my dogs, Barnabas and Bailey, an Alaskan malamute and malamute/wolf who were two of my closest companions. We walked along a mountain stream that whispered the gentle voice of serenity and peace while echoing the power and beauty of the golden aspens that kissed the sky and blended with the white clouds and crisp clean air. Barnabas and Bailey were good prayer partners. They, too, listened to the gentle sounds that surrounded us while I learned to listen to the still small voice of the Spirit who longed for union with my soul.

I learned in Flagstaff that God likes to speak to the children God created, including me. I was enjoying what Brother Lawrence talks about in his book *Practicing the Presence of God.* I learned from Brother Lawrence that the presence of God was something I could be aware of if I tuned my ear and my heart to God's abiding presence. I began to hear God's voice, and I began to long for more living water for my thirsty soul.

A few years later, a seminary class introduced me to the concept of this living water as able to satisfy the deepest longings of my heart... for love, acceptance, and the presence of God, who wants to give me life and heal my broken heart. I learned that I was broken, and I was beginning to experience the Love my soul had always longed for.

My athletic success began when I was seven years old. My softball team won the city championship, and my dad ran out onto the field with a huge smile and wide-open arms to embrace my victory and the fact that I hit the winning home run and pitched the final strikeout. This seems like a good metaphor for sharing an aspect of my story. My dad was a good man. He loved all five of his children the best way he knew how. The fact that he was an only child born to immigrant parents who didn't express emotion created awkwardness in my father with telling his kids how much he loved us. So, when my dad ran out onto the field when I was seven, I learned that I can receive love when I win games, hit home runs, and strike out the final batter. Until I walked into the seminary classroom, I didn't realize that the little girl who was hurting inside of me was desperately trying to recreate the scenario on the softball field every chance I got. The little girl living inside of me was desperately trying to meet her need for love the only way she knew how ... earning love, impressing people, and continuing to try to hit home runs.

In the seminary class I learned about the presence of the Spirit that can bring healing to past painful memories. A counselor facilitated a prayer session where the pain of not feeling loved by my dad as a little girl began to be exposed. For the first time, I felt the intensity of emotion well up from inside my soul and burst forth through my tears. The counselor gently helped me focus on Jesus, who could be present in a memory that revealed the source of an aspect of my broken soul, and I felt God's love in a way I never thought possible. The following years consisted of continuing to experience God and others in ways that began to satisfy the deep longings of my soul for love, while restoring places of neglect and hurt that prevented me from experiencing life to the full. Now I facilitate similar experiences with others who are learning they are broken and are longing to be loved and feel accepted by God.

Linda was a twenty-four-year-old seminary student, studying to prepare herself to minister among street kids in Latin America. Born to missionary parents, Linda served God all her life and taught children both at her church and in an art school in her community. Linda also loved to dance and could be found dancing the salsa at a local nightclub two to three times per week. Because she was an attractive woman, men invited her to dance on a regular basis, and often the invitation to dance was followed by an invitation to go home together, which Linda had a hard time resisting. This pattern was what brought her to meet with me for spiritual direction and to experience Visio Divina. Her struggle was a secret one. She continued to take classes at seminary and teach classes at her church when all the while she was sleeping with men she barely knew.

When I first met Linda she was struggling with guilt and shame because of the choices she was making. Her prayer life was nonexistent, and she had difficulty reading the Bible. She loved God and was grieved that she wasn't able to live according to her values of sexual purity. In one of our first sessions together, Linda expressed that she knew in her head that God loved her, but was having a hard time experiencing that love in her heart. In other words, her head knowledge about God wasn't able to override the deep emotions of her heart — guilt, shame, and a feeling that she did not deserve God's love.

Normally when I am meeting with someone for spiritual direction I listen for what might be the deeper cries and longings of the heart that lie beneath a person's struggle. As I was listening to Linda, I began to hear that at the core of her struggle she didn't feel loved by God. When I begin to hear a specific heart cry or longing, I make a mental note of it, and when it's time to pray, that cry or longing of the heart becomes the basis of our focus in Visio Divina. After Linda shared her story, I asked if it would be okay if we spent some time being quiet with God asking Him to help her understand why she didn't feel loved by Him. After a few minutes of silence, I heard Linda say,

I see an image of Jesus. He is standing over me. I am sitting on the ground. I am wearing dirty clothes. My face is dirty, and I am cowering away from him. He is just standing there. He is reaching down to pick me up, but I am afraid. Karen asks me if I can see his eyes. I look at his eyes, and I see compassion. He wants to pick me up. I let him. He gently touches me, and then he picks me up. As he holds me, my dirty clothes aren't dirty anymore. He put a red robe on me. He has a smile on his face. I also look happy.

After her first experience of Visio Divina, Linda gradually began to *experience* deep in her heart that God really does love her and wants to be with her even when she feels dirty from the consequences of the choices she is making. During the next few months Linda gradually began to see and experience herself as accepted and loved by God.

In subsequent Visio Divina sessions, Linda continued to experience God through the opened eyes of her heart, God with her in a place she felt dirty and unlovable. This image of God's presence with her revealed by the Spirit also revealed Jesus to her. Jesus picks her up, washes her off and clothes her with a red robe. The image also reveals that God is not only able to be with us when we are dirty, but smiles when we let him love us.

As happened with Linda, God encounters us in prayer, and many such stories are recorded in scripture. For example, in an experience of Visio Divina Linda recalls Adam and Eve's experience with God in the Garden of Eden as narrated in Genesis 2:4–3:24. This well-known story, which resonates with people of many faith traditions, has been made into countless movies, books, songs, paintings, and poems, all intended to capture and communicate the various meanings of this complex yet simple story.

As you know, after their creation, Adam and Eve were hanging out with God in the Garden. God told them that they could enjoy everything that God had made: the fruit of the trees, the beauty of creation like sunsets and waterfalls, and even the animals that Adam actually got to name. The only thing God told them not to do was eat the fruit from one of the trees called the tree of the knowledge of good and evil. It really doesn't matter whether we know what that actually means. What matters is that God gave Adam and Eve the entire garden to play in, take care of, and benefit from. There were relationships with God and each other to enjoy, food to eat, work to be done, and adventures to have. However, as an expression of God's love for them, God told them not to eat from this particular tree in the garden, knowing that the fruit from that tree would not be good for them. Indeed, God told them, if they ate that fruit, they would die.

Almost everyone knows what happened next. Adam and Eve ate the fruit after a serpent enticed and tricked Eve into believing that eating the fruit would actually be a good thing, and that she would gain wisdom. The story climaxes when, after eating the fruit, Adam and Eve run away and hide. The story goes like this. . . .

> They [Adam and Eve] heard the sound of the Lord God walking in the garden at the time of the evening breeze, and the man and his wife hid themselves from the presence of the Lord God among the trees of the garden. But the Lord God called to the man, and said to him, "Where are you?" He said, "I heard the sound of you in the garden, and I was afraid, because I was naked; and I hid myself." He said, "Who told you that you were naked? Have you eaten from the tree of which I commanded you not to eat?"
> — Genesis 3:8–11

Another interesting part of this story is that prior to eating the fruit from the tree, "they were both naked and were not ashamed," but after eating the fruit, Adam said, "I heard the sound of you in the garden, and I was afraid, because I was naked; and I hid myself." Something seems to have happened to them during their interaction with the serpent and eating the fruit that caused them to be afraid of God, hide, and feel ashamed.

### *Visio Divina*
### *Five movements for*
### *entering into God's presence*

1. *Find a quiet place where you won't be distracted.*

2. *Begin to empty your mind of distracting thoughts and concerns.*

   ◆ *Write down everything that you are concerned about and what needs to be done today.*

   ◆ *Release the list to God, who will hold it for you while you are praying.*

   ◆ *Ask God to enable you to enter into a place of rest, a rest that will enable your heart and mind to come to a place of quiet (Hebrews 4:1–3).*

   ◆ *Meditate on a cross or another symbol that will help you begin to focus on God.*

3. *After you begin to feel quiet and focused on God, read Ephesians 1:17–19 or pray that prayer for yourself. Ask God to open the eyes of your heart, enabling you to see what God wants you to see.*

4. *Be open to allow images, thoughts, impressions, and feelings to come into your conscious awareness. If you continue to feel distracted, go back to step 2.*

5. *If an image comes into your mind with a corresponding feeling of peace, ask the Spirit to show you where God is in the image. Remain quiet, focused on the image as it is revealed. Begin to sink into the experience of God being with you. Let yourself feel the image, sinking deeper and deeper into the experiential reality of God's presence with you.*

*If you are concerned about what you are experiencing or wonder whether you are making it up, you can ask God to quiet your own voice and any other voices that you might be hearing. You can say something like, "God, please quiet my own voice. I only want to experience what the Spirit who reveals God would like me to experience."*

The similarity between this story about the Garden of Eden and Linda's experience becomes evident when we take a look at the interaction between Adam, Eve, and God and compare it to Linda's relationship with God. Adam and Eve do something that God tells them not to do. They eat the fruit. After they eat the fruit God finds them hiding, afraid. Linda is doing something that she

believes God has told her not to do, sleeping with men
to whom she hasn't made a commitment. In her experience of Visio Divina, God finds Linda, who is cowering
away, afraid, just as in the Garden of Eden God pursues
Adam and Eve following their choice of disobedience,
finds them, and clothes them with garments to cover their
nakedness. Linda's experience of Visio Divina, God pursued Linda, too, and also clothed her with a garment, a
red robe. Adam, Eve, and Linda were all three fearful of
God, but Adam, Eve, and Linda were all found by God
and experienced that they did not need to be afraid. God
loved them and clothed them when they may have ex-
pected punishment. It seems to me that they experienced
what John writes about in the New Testament. There is
no fear in love, but perfect love casts out fear, because
fear has to do with punishment (1 John 4:18).

## *What do you think?*

The following questions may be helpful in getting started
if you decide to journal your thoughts and feelings.

1.  Adam, Eve, and Linda experienced God accepting
    them following their choice of disobedience. What
    does that tell you about God?

2. How does Linda's story connect with your story?

3. Which part of Linda's story triggered the strongest feelings in you?

4. What do you think about Ephesians 1:17–19 and this whole thing about seeing images through the opened eyes of your heart?

5. What questions do you still have?

# TWO

# PRESENCE

*Can I expect God to love me
in a tangible way?*

As I described in chapter one, Visio Divina opens our heart and mind to an experiential encounter with God and thereby enables us to feel loved by God in a tangible way. When we experience God encountering us during Visio Divina, we experience God in our emotions and our imagination through all of our senses.

A tangible experience of God's real presence is what Melissa was seeking as she came to spiritual direction struggling to know whether God really loved her. She *believed* God loved her, meaning she had a kind of head knowledge of God, but she was struggling to *feel* God's love. She described God as feeling very distant. She had been a Christian for many years, read her Bible on a regular basis, and attended church most Sunday mornings. She came to spiritual direction because one of her friends shared her experience of God through Visio Divina. Melissa had never experienced an image of God during prayer and was very skeptical that God would love her in any way.

After meeting with Melissa for a few weeks, getting to know her better, and introducing her to the concept of Visio Divina, we started to spend a portion of our time together doing Visio Divina. We began by sitting together quietly. I gently invited God to help her enter into a place of rest, a place where her mind and heart would be quiet. I invited her to release to God any distracting thoughts that entered her mind, suggesting that God would hold them during our time together. After a few minutes, Melissa began to experience a place of quiet and rest. I asked the Spirit to open the eyes of her heart so that Melissa could come to know God better. I invited God to reveal to her how God wanted to love her. We continued to sit quietly together for a few more minutes and then Melissa began to share.

> I see a hospital room. My mom is in bed. My family is there. Jesus is holding me as an infant. I was just born. My mom is looking away. Jesus' hand looks like a woman's hand. His hand is on my chest. His hair is long. All Jesus' features are really feminine. His long white

doctor's coat is now a dress. Jesus is now a woman. She is singing to me. There is a basin full of water. She starts cleaning me and then dries me off with a big fluffy towel. She wraps me in a blanket and holds me close. She is holding me so close I can feel her heart beating. She is patting me on the back. My mom rolls over to look at me but then rolls back over and looks away. She seems depressed. Jesus and I sit down in a rocking chair. She is looking in my eyes. She is smiling at me. I can see the love in her face, but there is something more, kind of like awe. She is amazed at her father's creation. I feel nice.

*Can a woman forget her nursing child, or show no compassion for the child of her womb? Even these may forget, yet I will not forget you.* — Isaiah 49:15

These words, written to the people of Israel exiled in Babylon, speak of God's compassion directed toward a people who feel forgotten by that same God. God speaks through the prophet Isaiah of Babylon, reminding the people that even if a mother forgets her nursing child, God, as a good mother, will show compassion and not forget her children. The biblical imagery of God as a nursing mother helps us reflect on God's feminine essence and desire to be our mother. Indeed, the psalmist reveals to us what it is like to rest in God's feminine, compassionate love. "I have stilled and quieted my soul; like a weaned child with its mother, like a weaned child is my soul within me" (Psalm 131:2).

During Visio Divina Melissa experienced an image of herself when she was an infant[1] and in this image she began to see how her mother wasn't able to show her how much Melissa was loved, because Melissa's mother suffered from depression when she was born. Melissa entered into a world where her primary caregiver was physically present but not able to be lovingly present to her daughter.

In this experience of Visio Divina, God revealed herself as willing and able to come to Melissa as an infant, revealing how much she loves Melissa, as a mother loves her nursing child. As Jesus held the infant, Melissa told me she could feel her heartbeat and described how peaceful she felt in her arms. I then invited Melissa to sink into the image, to let go, as much as possible, into the feelings

---

1. Recent research on infant attachment theory articulated by Allan N. Schore, a member of the clinical faculty at UCLA Geffen School of Medicine and author of *Affect Dysregulation and Disorders of the Self* and *Affect Regulation and the Repair of the Self*, reveals that an infant's brain stores experience as implicit memory during the first year of life. These experiences cannot be consciously recalled as explicit memory, but shape the developing self. During Visio Divina these implicit memories seem to be revealed as images that represent relational patterns of interaction between the infant and the caregiver.

of being held, feeling safe, feeling wanted, and feeling the heartbeat of God as mother. We sat together in silence for ten minutes, as Melissa sank more and more deeply into the experience of God's love for her, going to a place in her soul where her mother's lack of love had been internalized. In subsequent weeks, Melissa and I sat together while God continued to meet her in this place within her soul, helping her to feel the heartbeat of comfort and safety, the tangible experience of God's love.

Eventually, Melissa began to feel secure in the strength of God's love holding her as an infant, at which point she began to feel the pain of her mother's depression and her inability to love her newborn baby. In grieving the loss of her mother's love, Melissa began a journey of healing, one that helped her understand why it was difficult for her to experience being loved by others. As we continued this prayer practice for many weeks, she gradually began to feel joy while being held by God, while she herself nurtured and played with the little baby who longed to be loved.

As Melissa was being held by God, the mother who loved her, she began to connect to emotions of comfort, safety, security, and eventually joy. A psychological theory of infant development called attachment theory, developed by John Bowlby and Mary Ainsworth, and expanded by many other researchers, such as Allan Schore and Daniel Siegel currently helps us understand the importance of a primary caregiver, usually a mother, providing emotional regulation for an infant. Emotional regulation simply means the mother helps a baby feel; a baby cannot feel without the presence of a mother. When a baby feels the love of a mother, those feelings are internalized as "I am loved." Unfortunately, a baby also internalizes other emotions from the mother, such as "I am unlovable" when a mother is not able to share emotions of love with her baby. If a mother rejects her baby, the baby grows up feeling and fearing rejection from others. Melissa had a hard time experiencing love from others and from God. She felt God was distant, maybe similar to her mother feeling distant while she struggled with depression. As God began to re-parent Melissa, she began to feel emotions of being loved. When a baby feels joy, she is feeling the joy of her caregiver. Melissa felt both loved by her heavenly mother and she felt God's joy in her presence.

## *What do you think?*

The following questions may be helpful if you decide to journal your thoughts and feelings.

1. How does Melissa's story connect with your story?

2. Which part of Melissa's story triggered the strongest feelings in you?

3. Read Isaiah 49. What do you think about the idea that God is like a nursing mother?

4. What questions do you have?

# THREE

# OPENNESS

*How do I learn how to be open to love?*

The cry of humanity's heart is to love and to be loved. Created with the capacity to give and receive love, we reflect in our loving nature God's own character and the embodiment of God's essence. Whenever we love, it is God's presence loving through us, enabling us to love.

If we all are born with the potential and the capacity to love and be loved, why are we so bad at it? When I look around our world, I honestly don't see a lot of love going around. Ethnic cleansing, war, terrorism, poverty, racism, sexism, oppression, abuse, violence, environmental degradation, abortion, homophobia, exploitation, depression, suicide, hate crimes, and many, many other reflections of our lack of ability to love abound in our world. It makes me think of Rodney King, made famous by the Los Angeles Watts Riots, and his statement, "Why can't we all just get along?" Rodney's question prompts me to ask, "Why do we have such a hard time loving God, loving our neighbor, and loving ourselves?"

One example from my own life suggests some answers. In 1991, I led a successful ministry event for women in athletics. Female athletes and coaches from all over the United States attended this first-ever national conference organized for the purpose of offering encouragement for female leaders who had influenced many in their careers as athletes, coaches, and athletic administrators. Many of the women who came to the conference were struggling with whether God had called them to be a leader. They loved God and desired to serve God with their lives, but had often been told by the churches they attended that women can't lead within the church, which caused an internal conflict for most of them. Why can a woman lead in ministries such as coaching and not lead in ministries such as the church? So the purpose of this weekend was to offer encouragement and affirmation to these women and their call as Christian leaders. In their feedback, many of the women who attended reported that the weekend did just that for them, and overall the event was successful.

The day after, however, I cried uncontrollable tears of sadness and grief as the weekend had been a success, yet I myself felt unaffirmed and unloved. Of all the days, this should have been one day when I felt good about myself. After all, I had just directed the *first-ever* national conference for women in athletics after only having been on staff with this ministry for nine months. My boss told me no one in the history of our organization had ever done something like this in their first year of ministry. I had been invited to meet with the national leaders to evaluate the conference. I was recognized. Women were encouraged. So, why, the day after, was I crying? Why did I feel so empty on the inside? This successful event, it seemed, only functioned to highlight my deep longing for something more than "success" or "recognition."

I came to realize that my tears meant that being recognized by others wasn't what I really longed for. I longed to be loved. Being seen by others as "spiritually gifted" didn't really make me feel loved. And then, I thought, what about all those people I used along the way so my ministry would be successful? How many people did I hurt as I quickly ascended the ladder of "ministry success?" How could I so easily use people, rather than really love *them?* How could I be insensitive to the needs of my friends and family as I worked 80 hours per week? And how did my vision of ministry success supersede the simple directive of loving God, loving my neighbor, and loving myself? My friends and family certainly didn't feel loved by me. One friend actually told me I seemed to be married to my job, and told me how much I had hurt him in prioritizing my ministry success over his friendship. Other friends told me after the conference that they felt used because the focus turned to me and my success rather than my sincerely acknowledging that they had been the conference: all of us women feeling affirmed and encouraged by the God who loves us.

In contrast to this and many other examples of how my limitations in feeling loved by God, myself, and others created within me significant difficulty in loving others, my journey of experiencing God through Visio Divina helped me to learn how to open myself up to love and to be loved. As I began to experience God revealing deep places of pain in my heart, I learned that the little girl inside of me was trying to earn love by continuing to be successful. I wouldn't have said it then, but now I realize how my personality and the charisms of grace enabled me to envision and direct a national conference, all the while the part of me that felt unloved kept me at a distance, closed down emotionally to those I worked with, prioritizing event success over loving and being loved by the people I serve. The little girl on the softball field was still trying to hit home runs to get Daddy's attention. Her unmet longing to be loved contributed to my using the women God wanted to love through me. In addition, those deep unmet longings for love contributed to my using the ministry to try to feel loved. I was no longer addicted to food. I was addicted to success.

Thankfully, because of Visio Divina, I learned that doing ministry and being recognized as successful wasn't the deepest longing of my soul. I was longing to feel loved; the little girl was tired of hitting home runs. She wanted to crawl into Daddy's lap and know that she didn't have to do anything to earn his love. During the past thirteen years I've experienced that I can crawl into God's lap and know that I am loved, and as a result I think I am better at loving others.

How we love is unique to our personhood, the unique experiences that shape us, and the way God desires to reveal God's self through us. Our personhood consists of who we are in the totality of our being. Our temperament and personality are expressions of our personhood; they influence the way we love. Experiences that shape us, such as early childhood relationships, also significantly contribute to how we love. In addition, God's Spirit in and working through us in ways that fulfill God's purposes for us shapes our longing for and expression of love.

The essence of our personality is something we're born with. It doesn't primarily change based on our experiences. It emerges over time and yet can be suppressed and damaged by neglect and a painful childhood. Our temperament is also something that develops over time, yet can be changed by experiences. One way of thinking about temperament is to describe how we are in the world in terms of four pairs of opposites, understood as temperament types: introverted or extroverted, thinking or feeling, sensing or intuitive, judging or perceiving.[1] Introduced by Carl Jung in 1921, temperament tests were later developed to help us understand our dominant temperament style,[2] indicating both areas of strength and growth. How we love and how open we are to being loved is influenced by our temperament, but our temperament isn't static and fixed. As we grow toward wholeness, our temperament can — and indeed must — change.

Early childhood relationships also shape how we give and receive love. If we grew up in families with parents who experienced perfect love and openness, then there is a good chance that we benefited from an inheritance of perfect love and openness that enables us to pass this perfect love and openness on to our children and to subsequent generations. The reality, though, is that there

---

1. For more information on temperament types, see David Keirsey and Marilyn Bates, *Please Understand Me: Character and Temperament Types* (Del Mar, CA: Prometheus Nemesis, 1984).

2. The Myers-Briggs Type Indicator is a helpful test to begin to understand your own temperament type.

isn't a perfectly loved human being among us, let alone a perfectly loved human being who found another perfectly loved human being with whom she chose to have children. In light of this reality, we all struggle, at least a little bit, with love, how to receive it and how to give it. Since our parents didn't experience perfect love, they had no way of loving us perfectly. Since we didn't experience perfect love, we have no way of loving our children perfectly. One aspect of our journey, therefore, is learning how to love, learning how to open ourselves up to love in ways not offered to us as children.

The greatest commandment is to love God with all our heart and all our mind and to love our neighbor as our self. If we weren't loved very well during our childhood, it is really hard to feel that we are loved as we grow into adulthood. If we don't feel like we are loved, we usually — unfortunately — do end up loving our neighbor the way we love our selves, that is to say, poorly. When we aren't able to love our neighbor, we are usually not able to love ourselves either. If we've been rejected as a child, we'll have a hard time loving and accepting our self and will continue to fear being rejected as an adult. Our inability to love and accept ourselves will contribute to our having difficulty loving and accepting others, especially those who remind us of the person who initially rejected us or a place inside us that we are rejecting. As a result of feeling rejected, we struggle with loving ourselves and subsequently struggle with loving others. God's Spirit in us and working through us can shape that particular aspect of faith that has to do with our openness to love.

Because we are all created in the image of God, God's presence loves through us and God's character is revealed when we love. Among the specific charisms of grace mentioned in the Bible is hospitality (Romans 12:13). When God's loving essence is revealed through hospitality, people feel welcomed and served by the person who enjoys loving people by opening his or her home, offering a warm meal, and creating an environment where people feel as if they have come home. When charisms of grace are expressed through God's people, people experience love, the essence of God's character.

One person may reflect God's loving presence by treating the poor and marginalized with dignity and respect, contributing to economic justice. Another person may reflect God's loving presence by ruling with authority, justice, humility, and compassion. A leader who reveals God's loving essence would embody God's love in his or her leadership choices. Another person may reflect God's desire for all people to experience a life of worth and therefore may advocate for those in our world who are being mistreated, abused, used, and exploited. Yet another person may reflect God's love as healer, offering herself and as a conduit of healing grace, mercy, and compassion for those who are suffering.

## *What do you think?*

The following questions may be helpful as you journal your thoughts and feelings.

1. What are some ways your parents helped you learn how to love?

2. What part of my story connected with yours?

3. Are you struggling to learn how to love?

4. What are some ways your parents contributed to your struggle?

5. Take a few moments now to enter into God's rest. Ask God to open the eyes of your heart, revealing to you a source of your struggle in being able to love _____. (See page 42 for a reminder of how to experience Visio Divina on your own).

FOUR

# ſTILLNEſſ

*How can I get to know the Goð
I am ſuppoſeð to truſt?*

Be still and know that I am God (Psalm 46:10). In quietness and trust is your salvation. In returning and rest
is your hope. Be still. Be quiet. Return. Rest. In our
fast-paced world of new ideas, new technologies, new
theologies, and new spiritualities, can we still trust the
saints of old who wrote these words? Be still and know
that I am God. In repentance and rest is your salvation,
in quietness and trust is your strength (Isaiah 30:15).

How difficult it is to be still, to be quiet, to return, and
to rest. What would our world be like if we all were able
to be still and know God, to be quiet and to experience
our being saved from our inability to love, to return to
our home as revealed in story of the Garden of Eden, and
to rest in the completed cosmic work of God; participating in the death and resurrection of Christ? This way of

stillness is Visio Divina. When we are still we begin to know God. In quietness we learn to trust God and begin to experience salvation. The God who rescues, rescues us from our limited ability to love and be loved. In returning, we position ourselves toward the garden, toward what God created, and, there we learn what we've lost and what we long for.

The garden is full of life, and we long for life. The garden is full of love, and we long for love. The garden is full of mutual and mutually beneficial relationships. Before the choice of disobedience, Adam and Eve were good stewards of the environment, and the environment in turn provided food. Adam and Eve worked in the garden, and as they worked, God provided for all their needs. Adam and Eve lived in unbroken union with God, and even after their choice of disobedience, this union, though severed for a time, was restored, for Adam and Eve continued to talk with God, hear God's voice, and enjoy God's presence. In reorienting ourselves toward the garden, we see and feel there what we long for, and in seeing and feeling our longing, we feel our full humanity. As we rest, we participate in the completed cosmic work of God, the death and resurrection of Christ. We experience God's love and are invited to trust in this God who created the garden full of love and life and who continues to re-create and restore within us our ability to live in the garden. God's love makes a way for us to come home, learning to love and experience life more fully.

How do I get to know the God I am supposed to trust? Obviously, God can be known through many different forms and structures, and God's presence is mediated through many different sacraments. God's presence is revealed in creation as well as through the scriptures. God's love is revealed when the poor are treated with dignity and respect and when authentic expressions of compassion are experienced by those who are hurting and suffering. God's presence is everywhere and is revealed when life is created and love is experienced. The purpose of this book is to introduce one way of getting to know God. So we can know and experience God in many different ways, including but not limited to an experience of God through Visio Divina.

Trusting God is very different from merely observing God in nature, or reading about God in scripture, or seeing God at work in our world through acts of compassion and justice. Trusting God assumes an interaction that fosters trust. Trusting in an idea or a concept is very different from trusting in a person who has earned our trust. Trusting in words about God isn't the same as trusting God. How can we trust someone we do not know? In order to trust we must be in a relationship with someone who is trustworthy. So, how is God earning your trust? Are you putting yourself in places where God can act to earn your trust? Visio Divina is one way we can open ourselves to a fuller experience of God, and in this experience we learn how to trust God and may also learn why we have such a hard time trusting.

Mary was twenty-nine years old when I met with her for spiritual direction. She was currently meeting with a psychotherapist and expressed a desire to include God more intentionally in her healing journey. She said she was feeling like God "wasn't there," and was struggling to trust Him. Mary's biological father committed suicide when she was nine. She struggled with feeling abandoned much of her life. Her journey consisted of meeting with me on a weekly basis for over a year, during which time she was studying in seminary, trying to discern God's call for her life and also struggling to believe that God was there for her in the midst of her pain.

I began to explain the concept of Visio Divina to Mary, communicating that it is one way of creating space for God and for us to become more conscious of God's presence with us. I explained that sometimes people begin to experience images, feel a sensation, hear an internal voice, or just feel quiet and at rest. Any experience is okay, and God is present even in the silence. Mary seemed to feel relieved that there was no expectation from me that she would experience something. When I said, "Visio Divina is all about grace, all you have to do is be present and open," she seemed to relax, which helped her experience God. This is her experience.

> During a Visio Divina session, I experienced an image of God as a knight in armor being my protector as a little girl. I was about nine years old. He followed me and was by my side at a family Christmas gathering. I then saw myself as a little girl in a gown of gold. I felt like a princess. Precious, loved, a guarded and protected treasure.
>
> In my experience of Visio Divina thus far, I have several times had the impression that God wanted me to turn to a particular passage of scripture that would further deepen his insight and guidance to me. As I was driving home from this session, scripture passages came to mind: ones I was not familiar with but anxiously looked up when I got home. (When I have these "impressions" I admit to feeling like I am running the risk of looking up a verse that reads, "the fig fell eight feet from the tree," or something similar!) After this especially meaningful prayer time, the Lord led me to the book of Psalms. The passage was Psalms 44–45.

> *Rouse yourself! Why do you sleep, O Lord? Awake,*
> *do not cast us off forever!*  — Psalm 44:23

> *Rise up, come to our help. Redeem us for the sake of*
> *your steadfast love.*  — Psalm 44:26

While reading Psalm 44 I felt so deeply that I could identify with this prayer for help and with the feeling that God had abandoned his people in hard circumstances.

> *For we sink down to the dust; our bodies cling to the*
> *ground.*  — Psalm 44:25

How deeply I connect with this feeling of having fallen into a pit with no one there to rescue me. In this place, this feeling of being left alone, it is so comforting to see the Lord walking by my side as a little girl being protected by a knight. It is also comforting to know that I am not the only one who has felt fear, has felt alone, and has felt frustration towards God for seeming to not be there. With more certainty and understanding, I came to believe he is there and that he is the protecting presence in my life.

Amazingly, as I read on to Psalm 45, I saw a picture of the church and his children as the bride being led into a royal wedding with the Lord. This picture of intimacy is a pure and striking symbol of God's undying love, affection

and commitment towards his people. I was moved deeply,
however, when I read:

> *Daughters of kings are among your ladies of honor: at*
> *your right hand stands the queen in gold of Ophir.*
> *— Psalm 45:9*

He loves me and is speaking to me! We are precious in
his sight. I read on:

> *The princess is decked in her chamber with gold-woven*
> *robes: in many-colored robes she is led to the king;*
> *behind her the virgins, her companions, follow.*
> *— Psalm 45:13b–14*

This image of wearing a golden gown is now very precious
to me, as I believe it was the Lord using ancient biblical
imagery to speak to me. This gown of gold is draped
by Jesus upon his children, and as a single woman it is
especially meaningful to me to feel that I am his bride,
committed to him and loving him my whole life.

> *Gird your sword on your thigh, O mighty one, in your*
> *glory and majesty.                    — Psalm 45:3*

These words have also confirmed the image of God as my
knight, my protector, my beloved, as I am his. Truly God
speaks in many ways to reach his loved one!

In Visio Divina Mary experienced a revelation of God as a strong, protective presence. Every nine-year-old little girl wants to see her daddy as a knight in shining armor, able to protect and love his little princess. As God revealed himself to Mary, God talked to the frightened nine-year-old little Mary who was abandoned by her father when he committed suicide. How can you trust someone who isn't there? Mary needed to experience God in this painful memory in order for her to begin to trust that God *was* in fact there for her, understanding her difficultly in trusting Him and being present with her in a way that begins to earn her trust.

Michael provides another example of a person learning to trust God through Visio Divina. In his own words:

As Karen and I waited in silence, I began to see an image come into my mind. I saw myself as an infant in a crib being picked up by a woman who held me and loved me. I saw my mom in another room. She was not responding to my cry. She and my dad were yelling at each other. They often did that. I sensed the woman who picked me up was Jesus, and then I experienced Jesus breast-feed me! After initially feeling surprised and unsure of what I was experiencing, I gradually felt comforted, totally peaceful and able to rest in her arms of love for me. From this experience and others in Visio Divina, God has been working in me an awareness of his love. I am learning how to trust.

Many of my directees tell me how God holds them as an infant during Visio Divina. As we enter into prayer, they see an image of themselves as an infant in a crib, crying, with their parent(s) not responding to their cries. I ask them to see where God is, and they respond by saying, "He is coming into the room, picking me up, and holding me." When I ask how it feels, they often say, something to the effect, "I feel really good, calm, peaceful, comforted." When I ask what they see, they often say, "I see his eyes. He loves me." Some even feel a heartbeat as God holds them. In these experiences, God seems to be re-parenting the infant, enabling these people to see and feel God's mothering presence and therefore helping them learn to trust.

Mary and Michael experienced God encountering them in places within their soul where they had a hard time trusting. Their past painful experiences of their primary caregiver not being present and able to love affected their experience of God and God's trustworthiness. As they began to experience God being different from their caregiver, they began to experience that God is trustworthy. God encountering us in ways that help us trust is one way we begin to know God is different from our parents. God is experienced as real and separate from both our unconscious brokenness and our expectations of who God is. In other words, God is experienced as separate from ourselves yet able to encounter us in ways unique to ourselves. As we get to know the God who is separate yet present, we can learn to trust this Source of love.

## *What do you think?*

The following questions may be helpful as you journal your thoughts and feelings.

1. Is God earning your trust? If so, how?

2. In what ways are you struggling to trust God?

3. How does Mary or Michael's story connect with your story?

4. Which part of Mary or Michael's story triggered the strongest feelings in you?

5. Do you have questions?

# FIVE

# TRUST

*How can I learn to trust
if I've been abandoned?*

The divorce rate in America doubled between 1965 and 1979. Many members of Generation X grew up in these broken homes. Not all divorces resulted in a fragmented family life or with consequences that affect a child's ability to trust. But, unfortunately, many children who had to suffer through the reality of one of their parents leaving home resulted in deep unconscious questions of their ability to be loved. When a person has been abandoned, the experience can result in internalizing feelings that they did something wrong. If Mommy left when her child was two, the two-year-old can process that reality by believing that something must be wrong with her; otherwise, Mommy would have stayed.

When over 50 percent of a generation are victims of divorce, a large number of that generation question

whether they are worth loving, whether they are worth
a parent staying around. William Mahedy and Janet
Bernardi in their book *A Generation Alone: Xers Making
a Place in the World*, highlight the spiritual discipline of
trust being a crucial component of GenX spirituality.
They suggest that trust should not only be a characteris-
tic of GenX community, but GenXers who have not had
role models who have enabled them to trust should also
practice it as a spiritual discipline. One GenXer, whose
parents divorced when he was seven, said it well when
he said, "I wince every time my father says he loves me,
because surely he didn't love me enough."

Although not all divorces end with painful consequences for the children, many do. It is this hurt we
will discuss here, in terms of a generation who longs to
trust, but might not know how to do it in light of their
experience of being abandoned by one of their parents.

## *We Love Because Christ First Loved Us*

Sometimes it's hard to know how to love others when we
haven't been loved ourselves. Sometimes we do in fact
love others the way we have been loved ourselves. If we
grew up in a secure environment where love was given
readily, emotional needs of safety, security, and comfort

were given, and words of affirmation and love where
communicated, then we most likely have the ability to
give and receive love from others in the same way. When
we've been abandoned, on the other hand, we sometimes
doubt whether we can trust those who say they love us.
When we can't trust those who say they love us, it is difficult to let ourselves be free to love others in the way we
long to be loved. When we hold back, fearing commitment and avoiding intimacy, we prevent ourselves from
receiving the love we need, and we sabotage our ability
to offer love to others. In the reality of being abandoned,
with the internal scares it leaves behind, how do we learn
how to trust?

Jill came to spiritual direction trying to understand
why she was fearful that her boyfriend, Bob, was going
to leave her. She loved Bob, and she believed he loved
her. They had talked about marriage and were looking
forward to a future life together. Jill struggled with deep
feelings of fear and anxiety about whether Bob would be
able to commit to her and whether she felt like she was
worth his not choosing another woman over her. They
had dated for three years. During that time Bob was
faithful and committed to her. He rarely spoke of other
women, and yet every once in awhile Jill saw him looking
at other women, noticing how beautiful they were. This

made Jill doubt whether Bob would continue to choose to be with her when there were other women he could choose from. Jill knew there were many more women much more beautiful than she. This fear and anxiety began to interfere with her ability to choose to be married. She sought out spiritual direction and Visio Divina in hope that she would begin to understand why it was so hard for her to trust that Bob's commitment to her would be lasting. Jill struggled with being able to love the man she was in love with because she didn't know how to trust a man who said he loved her, would stay with her, being committed to her for the rest of her life. The reality of that fear and that inability to trust caused her to resist letting go and giving herself freely to love. For Jill, learning how to trust meant understanding the unconscious aspect of her soul that continued to live out the reality of her parents' divorce and her father's leaving when she was three. As we entered into Visio Divina, God began to reveal a memory of when her dad walked away from the house, leaving her and her mother to be on their own. Jill described the experience as follows:

I see myself as a little girl. I'm standing at the front door-way. I look sad. I see my dad walking away from me. I think he is leaving when my parents got divorced when I was three. I sit down on the floor. I am all alone. My mom is in the other room. I can hear her crying. I hear Karen ask, "Can you see God anywhere?" Then I see Jesus. He walked in the front door, and he is sitting down next to me. He put his arm around me. I don't feel so alone now. He is just sitting with me. He says it is okay to feel sad. He said my daddy loved me, but couldn't stay. He said it's not about me. He said it's not my fault. He said he loves me, and he'll never leave me nor forsake me (she starts to cry). I feel sad that my daddy left. Why did he leave me? Why did he leave my mom? A few minutes later, I hear Karen ask, "God, how do you want to continue to love your daughter?" I feel him close to me. He is just continuing to hold me as I cry. He says that he is my father, and he won't ever leave me. He wants me to begin to trust Bob. He said Bob is a good man.

### *Staying Balanced*

*Visio Divina can open you up to experiences that are wonderful and life changing. It is important to stay balanced in your walk with God and your life with others while learning how to do Visio Divina. Sometimes people begin to experience God in such wonderful ways that they begin to think that Visio Divina is the only part of life that God is really interested in. It is important to maintain relationships with others in community and practice other spiritual disciplines that ensure a balanced approach to God and life.*

*God speaks through lots of different ways, including scripture, people, creation, circumstances and events, tradition, music, books, and more. Visio Divina is only one way God chooses to speak to people. I believe it is a very important way, but it will be helpful to remember that it is only one of many ways God speaks.*

As Jill began to realize that her fear and anxiety about Bob not being able to commit to her was coming from a place within her that remembered the pain of feeling abandoned by her father when she was three, she began to be able to differentiate between Bob's action and her little girl who feared that she would be abandoned again if she trusted a man. Gradually, over the next few months, Jill and I continued to do Visio Divina while talking about ways she could begin to learn to trust Bob at deeper levels within her soul. She felt more grief and sadness as a result of the little girl within her grieving the loss of her real daddy, and there were more experiences with God that confirmed his love for her in a way that began to heal the deep feeling of her not being worth a man staying for. Jesus began to dance with her and she began to see herself as a beautiful little girl, Daddy's princess, special, and one in whom he delights. As God revealed the joy he experienced in her presence, Jill began to feel that she was lovable and that she deserved the love of a man who also thought she was special and experienced joy in her presence.

As Jill grieved the loss of her father's choosing to leave her when she was three, she no longer lived out of these unresolved emotions within her soul. She no longer experienced Bob through those unresolved emotions, and she was able to begin to experience Bob as separate from her father. When we do not grieve our losses, those losses continue to affect how we experience current reality and relationships. For Jill, grieving the loss of her daddy's departure, combined with the experience of God's tangible presence, enabled her to begin to trust another man's love.

## *What do you think?*

1. How does your story connect with Jill's story?

2. Which part of Jill's story triggered the strongest feelings in you?

3. What connections do you make between Jill's story and how you trust others?

4. Do you have questions?

# SIX

# EMBRACE

*Will God be with me in my mess?*

When Linda from chapter one walked into my office and sat down, she began to share with me how ashamed she felt for sleeping with many different men, none of whom was her husband. She expressed remorse and guilt as a result of feeling she was not glorifying God with her body. She desperately wanted to be free from this struggle and had tried many times to stop sleeping with men she did not know very well. In addition, she said she felt embarrassed and ashamed of her behavior because she was in seminary, studying to live and work among the world's urban poor. On Sunday mornings she taught children at her church while also participating in the praise and worship band. Her fear of being "found out" contributed to her not being able to be a member of a small group of friends. A bright student, earning "A's" in most of her classes, externally Linda seemed to have her life in order.

But internally she felt like her life was a mess, and she was struggling to believe that God still loved her.

Linda shared with me that her biggest fear was that she would be exposed: that she would be found out and publicly humiliated because of the hypocrisy of her lifestyle. She was concerned that if the institution where she was studying discovered her behavior, she would not receive a positive letter of recommendation for her next ministry position. These fears left Linda alone and isolated within her community of faith.

The following biblical story, the story of the woman caught in adultery, shows Jesus encountering her in the midst of a life that was rather messy.

*Then each of them went home, while Jesus went to the Mount of Olives. Early in the morning he came again to the temple. All the people came to him and he sat down and began to teach them. The scribes and the Pharisees brought a woman who had been caught in adultery; and making her stand before all of them, they said to him, "Teacher, this woman was caught in the very act of committing adultery. Now in the law Moses commanded us to stone such women. Now what do you say?" They said this to test him, so that they might have some charge to bring against him. Jesus bent down and wrote with his finger on the ground. When they kept on questioning him, he straightened up and said to them, "Let anyone among you who is without sin be the first to throw a stone at her." And once again he bent down and wrote on*

*the ground. When they heard it, they went away, one by one,*
*beginning with the elders; and Jesus was left alone with the*
*woman standing before him. Jesus straightened up and said*
*to her, "Woman, where are they? Has no one condemned*
*you?" She said, "No one, sir." And Jesus said, "Neither do*
*I condemn you. Go your way, and from now on do not sin*
*again."*                                    —John 7:53–8:11

Jesus does not publicly expose this woman to shame
and condemnation. Instead, Jesus focuses on the community and says to them, "Let anyone among you who is
without sin be the first to throw a stone at her." One way
I understand "sin" is to mean miss the mark and fail to
love, fail to love God, ourselves, or our neighbor. Jesus'
invitation to the community to look at themselves highlights his awareness that this woman's sin, her struggle
with loving and being loved, is no different than the sins
of each member of the community. Instead of disciplining
her in the way of the Old Testament law, Jesus positions
her within the community as an equal. She is no longer
exposed and humiliated: It is they who don't know how
to love her. Jesus' invitation for her community to embrace her is the result of an encounter where she is no
longer viewed as a woman to be condemned, rather she
is viewed as a woman who belongs in community with
others who are learning how to love.

Linda had been fearful that her sin, her struggle to learn how to be loved and to love others, would cause her to be publicly exposed. She had also been fearful that her community of faith would not accept her if they really knew what was going on in her personal life. She also struggled to believe that God still loved her. These factors contributed to her feeling ashamed of her behavior, isolated, and alone. As we continued our sessions, the following Visio Divina occurs to her.

One early image I experienced in Visio Divina was based on an experience of my father changing my diapers when I was just a few months old. Evidently my father was showing off to my uncle — trying to convince him that he was a macho dad, able to change diapers like a pro. I pooped all over the diaper table as soon as he removed the diaper, and needless to say he was embarrassed, and I felt he was ashamed of me. I saw myself in that moment, ashamed and embarrassed — essentially by my own humanity. From a bird's-eye-view, I could see Baby Linda lying face up surrounded by her mess, and the top of my dad's head and his hands as he tried to clean up — to remove the evidence of my shame. Baby Linda's body went white — as if she wasn't breathing anymore, like her spirit/will to live had left at that moment. Then I saw Jesus come and comfort me. He wasn't bothered by the mess — in fact, I don't know if he even saw it. He immediately started loving me — cooing, tickling, and laughing — just delighting to be in my presence. He swooped me off that changing table and breathed life back into me. I saw Baby Linda's body return to its normal pink color, as Jesus continued to sing songs of love and blessing over me as he held me to his chest and walked me around the room.

As Linda reflected on her experience she said,

I learned that I had essentially been living in shame my entire life. I've spent my life making excuses for my existence — terrified that someone may find out I'm a mere mortal. Whenever I would make a mistake, I flipped out, especially when someone discovered my mistakes — even if they were accidents, or unintentional. If people were unjust to me, I believe I deserved it: after all, I hardly deserved to take a breath on this planet. The week following this session, I experienced two instances where I stood up for myself — one in which I was wrongly accused of a mistake, and the other in which I was mistreated. Without thinking, I immediately responded in my defense. I couldn't remember a time in my life where I had stood up for myself on the fly like that. The healing prayer image had begun to break the power of shame in my existence. I now knew I had a place on this planet, and could ask others to treat me with dignity and respect.

## *Jesus Comes into the Mess*

Linda's experience in Visio Divina reveals Jesus coming to her as an infant in the middle of a mess. The mess was a normal part of being human. Her dad's reaction to the mess was what contributed to Baby Linda's feelings of shame and embarrassment. However, when Jesus comes in and picks Baby Linda up, delighting to be in her presence, an experience of being loved and therefore healed has occurred, for her mess does not bother Jesus. In fact Linda experiences that Jesus is concerned about her (not her mess) and loves her in such a way that the shame from this incident comes to be removed. Jesus holding Baby Linda, embracing her in the midst of her shame and mess, led to her feeling free from the shame from this incident.

In addition, Linda experienced Jesus coming to her in such a way that empowered her to believe, "I have a place on this planet and I can ask others to treat me with dignity and respect." Linda could return to her communities less fearful of being publicly shamed for the "mess" that she had begun to work through.

In the story of the woman caught in adultery, similar themes emerge. The scribes and Pharisees have plotted against both the woman and Jesus to expose her sin and to question Jesus' identity as the Messiah, exploiting this woman as an object for their personal ulterior motives. They are not treating her with dignity and respect until Jesus comes on the scene and challenges the patriarchal way of interacting with her, their view of her as a woman who can be used and then stoned. Jesus gives her dignity by exposing everyone's sin and inviting her to return to her community, to "go and sin no more." The encounter with Jesus may have contributed to her feeling like an equal, possibly resulting in her being able to stand up for herself, demanding that men treat her with dignity and respect.

Linda's encounter with Jesus in Visio Divina led her to see herself as a woman who deserves to be treated with dignity and respect, just as the woman's encounter with Jesus in scripture resulted in her being treated as an equal among others who are learning how to love. By not condemning her sin, Jesus leveled the playing field and returns this woman to the embrace of her community, equal to the scribes and Pharisees.

The empowerment to go and sin no more is what I believe is central to the process of transformation. In the midst of sin, which I define as missing the mark of love, feeling guilty and ashamed, God encounters us, accepts us, begins to show us why we struggle, and then begins to help us be free from our inability to love. Therefore, the process of transformation is one where God's grace is experienced right in the midst of our mess, accepting us, healing us and empowering us to love.

## *What do you think?*

1. How does your story connect with Linda's story?

2. Which part of Linda's story triggered the strongest feelings in you?

3. Are you feeling loved by God in the midst of your mess?

4. What do you think of the concept of sin to describe our inability to love?

### *Visio Divina and Scripture*

*Five passages of scripture have provided a helpful lens for understanding what God seems to be doing during Visio Divina. I summarize them here.*

## 1. Character of God (Genesis 2:4–3:24)

*In the garden story recorded in Genesis 2:4–3:24, we see that God pursues Adam and Eve immediately following their choice to eat the forbidden fruit. In pursuing them, God shows God's desire to continue to be in relationship, even after their choice. God talks and God walks with Adam and Eve. It is a common Christian view that sin separates us from God. This passage seems to communicate that God does the exact opposite. God is a loving God who pursues us and walks with us and talks with us — even when we make choices that go against God's commands.*

## 2. Ministry of the Servant of Yahweh (Isaiah 61:1–2a)

*"The Spirit of the Lord God is upon me, because the Lord has anointed me; he has sent me to bring good news to the oppressed, to bind up the brokenhearted, to proclaim liberty to the captives, and release to the prisoners; to proclaim the year of the Lord's favor."*

*This scripture speaks to the ministry of the servant of Yahweh that includes "binding up broken hearts" and "setting captives free." During Visio Divina people experience God binding up wounded hearts and bringing freedom to our soul.*

### 3. God's Love Poured into Our Hearts (Romans 5:5)

*"Hope does not disappoint us, because God's love has been poured into our hearts through the Holy Spirit that has been given to us."*

God's presence experienced through Visio Divina includes this love that is being poured into the hearts of the people in Rome. The love of God being poured into our hearts is a tangible presence that sometimes can be felt with our emotions and is experienced through prayer, resulting in a hope that does not disappoint.

### 4. Jesus as "Word of God" Revealing and Healing Motives of Our Heart (Hebrews 4:12)

*"Indeed, the word of God is living and active, sharper than any two-edged sword, piercing until it divides soul from spirit, joints from marrow; it is able to judge the thoughts and intentions of the heart."*

God's presence experienced through Visio Divina is able to divide soul from spirit, joint from marrow, and judge the thoughts and intentions of the heart. When you experience this piercing word of God, you are experiencing Jesus, the incarnate word of God (John 1:1), who is able to reveal and heal the broken-hearted.

## 5. Eyes of Our Heart Opened to Know God Better
## (Ephesians 1:17–19)

*"I pray that the God of our Lord Jesus Christ, the Father of glory, may give you a spirit of wisdom and revelation as you come to know him, so that, with the eyes of your heart enlightened, you may know what is the hope to which he has called you, what are the riches of his glorious inheritance among the saints, and what is the immeasurable greatness of his power for us who believe, according to the working of his great power."*

*During Visio Divina God's Presence is mediated to us through prayer. This prayer in Ephesians is for people to experience the spirit of wisdom and revelation as they come to know God. The prayer is that the eyes of their hearts would be enlightened so they would know the hope to which they are called and the riches of God's glorious inheritance. The eyes of our heart are central to experiencing God's hope and the richness of God's promises. Visio Divina enables the eyes of our hearts to be opened.*

# HOPE

## THE OPPOSITE OF HOPELESSNESS

What are we supposed to hope in? How can we experience hope in the midst of suffering? If perfect love removes fear, why does fear still prevent me from hope? I address these questions in the following section as I share stories of people whose experience of God through Visio Divina enabled them to have more hope.

# SEVEN

# DESPAIR

*What am I supposed to hope in?*

When I first met Yolanda, she told me she felt hopeless and was in despair. She had just completed the paperwork for a divorce from a husband who, although a Christian, physically abused her. She told me that she had also been abused by another man earlier in her life; a neighbor molested her when she was four years old and then told her not to tell anyone. Yolanda held this secret her entire life, denying it had caused her any harm.

Yolanda was successful in graduate school, on her way to becoming an ordained pastor, but also was struggling to overcome feelings of guilt and shame as a result of choosing divorce, since she believed divorce is not part of God's way. She came to spiritual direction seeking help. She told me she felt like she was bleeding on the inside and nothing she tried could stop the blood.

Desperate for hope, she nevertheless did not believe she could experience it.

During one of our times of Visio Divina, Yolanda tearfully shared the following experience.

> I felt that I had failed. I felt like I had a scarlet letter. I meant my marriage vows. I said them to God and I promised to do everything I could do. I promised to give everything, and it didn't work. But, then, I felt like God was saying, "I understand that you have done all you can do and I understand that you don't want to stay. I don't think that you have failed. I don't think of you any less."
>
> I just felt accepted by God and freed. That was wonderful.

During Visio Divina, Yolanda continued to experience God in ways that helped her feel loved and accepted, which eventually enabled her to begin to hope that the pain would one day go away. During a particularly painful week, she had the following Visio Divina.

> I see me on the ground in a desert. I feel like that is me emotionally. Now, I see the same desert, and Jesus is there filling me up with living water. I see the cross, and I see me under the cross. Jesus is telling me to just sit at the base of the cross. I see a river with green trees that

are lush. I hear "I will restore your soul." God is saying,
"I am your shepherd. I lead you by still waters and I am
restoring your soul."

Yolanda's story is similar to the biblical story of the
woman at the well who had many husbands (John 4:1–
42). The story shows Jesus encountering a woman who
was marginalized in her day, was not supposed to talk
with a Jewish man, and yet was given living water so she
would never be thirsty again. This is how John records
the story:

> *When a Samaritan woman came to draw water, Jesus said to*
> *her, "Will you give me a drink?" . . . The Samaritan woman*
> *said to him, "You are a Jew and I am a Samaritan woman.*
> *How can you ask me for a drink?" (For Jews do not associate*
> *with Samaritans.) Jesus answered her, "If you knew the gift*
> *of God and who it is that asks you for a drink, you would*
> *have asked him and he would have given you living water."*
> *"Sir," the woman said, "You have nothing to draw with and*
> *the well is deep. Where can you get this living water? Are*
> *you greater than our father Jacob, who gave us the well and*
> *drank from it himself, as did also his sons and his flocks and*
> *herds?" Jesus answered, "Everyone who drinks this water will*
> *be thirsty again, but whoever drinks the water I give him will*
> *never thirst. Indeed, the water I give him will become in him*
> *a spring of water welling up to eternal life."*
>
> *The woman said to him, "Sir, give me this water so that*
> *I won't get thirsty and have to keep coming here to draw*

*water." He told her, "Go, call your husband and come back."*
*"I have no husband," she replied. Jesus said to her, "You*
*are right when you say you have no husband. The fact is,*
*you have had five husbands, and the man you now have is*
*not your husband. What you have just said is quite true."*
*"Sir," the woman said, "I can see that you are a prophet."*
*                                                    — John 4:7–19*

Feminist New Testament scholar Luise Schottroff highlights the patriarchal culture in which the woman in the
biblical story lived: "The Samaritan woman probably had
a thoroughly typical woman's biography in patriarchy
behind her. Thus, she was a victim, or at most, a coopera-
tor — she understands herself as an agent in a patriarchal
system that oppressed women." Similarly, Yolanda experienced oppressive actions from her husband who did
not respect her. Indeed, both Yolanda and the woman at
the well were victims of patriarchy. And, yet, both also
experienced Jesus encountering them and offering them
a source of life for their thirsty soul. Yolanda had an
experience of God coming to her while she was feeling
hopelessness and despair, as she felt marginalized, oppressed, and broken. As Jesus encountered the woman
at the well and revealed how many husbands she had, he
encountered her in such a way that exposed her heart, but
instead of shaming, judging, condemning, or punishing

her, he invited her to taste the living water that would enable her to never be thirsty again.

What is this living water that Jesus promised would enable her to never be thirsty again? John Sanford, a Jungian analyst and well-known writer in the area of psychology, religion, and inner growth, provides a helpful understanding of the meaning of the metaphor of water. "The early church psychologist-theologians did not hesitate to identify this water with Christ, whom they termed 'the fountain of life.'" Sanford continues to explain the meaning of the metaphor by quoting an early church desert father, Clement of Alexandria, as a source of knowledge: "Speaking in his inimitable mystical, psychological way, Clement of Alexandria writes of water that not only is it the natural source of all life, so that 'without the element of water, none of the present order of things can subsist,' it is also a spiritual element without which the life of the soul cannot exist. In fact, this water is none other than 'Christ, the maker of all,' who came down as the rain and was known as a spring (John 4:14), diffused himself as a river (John 7:38) and was baptized in the Jordan. Christ is the boundless river that makes glad the city of God ... (Psalm 46:4), the illimitable Spring that bears life to all men and has no end, who is present everywhere and absent nowhere, who is incomprehensible to angels and invisible to human beings. He concludes with words that could well have been spoken to the Samaritan woman: 'When you hear these things, beloved, take them not as if spoken literally, but accept them as presented in a figure.' " This living water is the life-giving presence of God. God is love. Jesus offered this life-giving presence of God's love to both the woman at the well and to Yolanda.

Yolanda's encounter with God through Visio Divina is similar to Jesus encountering the woman at the well in yet another way. In meeting the woman at the well, Jesus challenged his own culture's expectation that women's role in society was to be silent in the presence of men. New Testament theologian Sandra Schneiders highlights that the woman at the well and Jesus had a genuine theological dialogue, and this radical encounter caused the woman to reflect on the identity of this man because of how he treated her as a woman, how he knew the motives of her heart, and how he loved her. In the end, he sends her forth as a partner in theological dialogue and empowered to be a leader in her community.

Yolanda's experience of Jesus loving her also caused her to reflect upon his identity. Yolanda's view of God changed from a dictator, standing back pointing the finger, ready to punish her when she did something wrong. Rather, God was revealed as a loving, immanent presence, able to help her understand the deeper motives of her heart that contributed to her choosing an abusive relationship to her husband. The grace that Yolanda received was a grace of self-knowledge and self-acceptance in the midst of her pain and feelings of hopelessness. Indeed, New Testament scholar Dorothy Lee summarizes the encounter of Jesus with the woman at the well in a similar way. The story "functions not to expose moral guilt but to uncover the pain and unrest of the woman's life. Through the self-knowledge gained by the woman, Jesus is revealed to her as the source of life, the giver of living water. The symbolism impels the woman, not toward moral rectitude, but toward a transformed understanding of herself, and her thirst for life." In a similar way, Yolanda experienced God's love, her source of life, which brought self understanding and gave her hope to live her life differently.

So, what are we supposed to hope in? I believe we are supposed to hope in love. When we are loved, hope grows within us. When we are alive enough to hope, we hope in someone being there for us, someone showing us that they care, someone who understands us, and someone who can help us continue to become the person we were created to be.

We want to be known. We want to be accepted. We want to know others. We want to accept others. We want the world to be a more loving place. The child in southern Asia who has been orphaned by the tsunami needs to hope that someone will love him; someone will be there for him, showing him that they care, understanding his hopelessness, and helping him through tangible expressions of love. The lonely husband who sacrificed many hours to provide for his family while his wife was having an affair needs to know that there is someone there for him, someone showing him that he cares by offering tangible expressions of love. Hope grows as we are encountered by love. Love can be offered and expressed in multifaceted ways. Visio Divina is one way we can be encountered by Love, and it's Love that helps us hope.

## *What do you think?*

1. How does your story connect with Yolanda's story?

2. Which part of Yolanda's story triggered the strongest feelings in you?

3. In what ways would you like to experience God's healing love so you can feel more hope?

4. How are you opening yourself to experience healing love? Is it time to meet with a spiritual director, pastoral counselor, or psychotherapist?

5. What questions do you have?

# EIGHT

# ∫UFFERING

*How can I experience hope
in the midst of suffering?*

Alan sought out spiritual direction and Visio Divina to try
to work through some struggles in his relationship with
God. To him, God was distant and unloving, and till we
met, Alan had never heard God's voice and didn't really
expect God to speak to him. He told me his fiancée heard
God's voice, and he wanted to know why God spoke to
her and not to him. He tried to listen to God on his own
but felt like he never heard anything. He also shared
with me a desire to understand himself better, especially
the impact that not knowing his biological father had on
his life. Raised by a single mother after his father abandoned them both at his birth, Alan expressed regret that
his dad never saw him play baseball or graduate from
college. After many painful experiences of missing his father, Alan realized he had become hard and tough, not

wanting to feel weak and vulnerable around people. But he also realized that a part of him wanted to feel like God was safe.

After a few weeks of meeting together for spiritual direction, Alan began to feel more comfortable with me and with Visio Divina as a prayer practice. Gradually he began to experience recurring images of how God's love was transforming his heart from a heart of stone to a heart of flesh. Following is his account of one of his experiences.

An image that has reoccurred in my experiences of Visio Divina has been my heart. The first time I experienced the image, I was able to see my heart held in the hands of God. It was anatomically correct, yet looked as though it were made of pumice stone, rather than flesh. It was clearly dark, cold, hard, and riddled with holes. As God held my stony heart, I saw God pour Love into my heart — God's essence filled every space with light. I felt warm. I felt loved. I knew that my hardened heart wasn't going to stay that way. I felt hope that I was going to be able to change.

*Suffering produces endurance, and endurance produces character, and character produces hope, and hope does not*

*disappoint us, because God's love has been poured into our*
*hearts through the Holy Spirit that has been given to us.*
                                        *— Romans 5:3b–5*

Though I struggle with the idea that God does not remove us from pain and suffering, I do see how God is
often revealed to us in and through our pain and suffering. In Romans, Paul speaks of hope as part of the
experience of suffering. Personally, I'd like God to take
pain away, but Paul, the author of Romans, shares a very
different perspective. He jolts his readers with a view that
suffering produces transformation, and in the midst of
suffering there can be an experience of God that offers
hope. Joseph Fitzmyer, a New Testament scholar, provides an illuminating interpretation of this love of God
that was poured into the hearts of those early Christians:
"The image is that of life-giving water being poured out
(Isaiah 44:3). Paul applies it to God's love, that is, the
divine energy manifesting itself in an overwhelming embrace of once godless creatures who are smothered with
his openness and concern for them. It is the manifesta-
tion of God's giving of himself without restraint, in a way
unparalleled by any human love. It is impossible for a
human being to imagine the dimensions or bounds of divine love: humanity knows of it only because God has

graciously willed to pour it out and make it known. Paul insists not simply that we become aware that God loves us, but that in the same experience we receive an assurance of God's love for us, a love that becomes the central motive of our own moral being: we love because he first loved us (1 John 4:19). Because the nature of God himself is love, in giving us love he imparts to us something of his own nature."

During Visio Divina, Alan experienced Love being poured into his heart, gradually transforming his heart of stone into a heart of flesh. In the midst of the pain of feeling distant from God, Alan sensed this divine energy embracing him and loving him.

When the suffering doesn't go away, God wants to be with us in it. Instead of looking at suffering as a punishment from God or a consequence of our bad behavior, suffering can be a place where we can most profoundly experience God's love. In part, suffering forces us to recognize our need for God, and in recognizing our need for God, we become more open to the source of all help. When we become more conscious of our need, and turn our focus toward God, God offers his presence, which can result in transformation and hope.

A simple application of Paul's message is that there is hope for those who are suffering. The hope that does not disappoint is realized because suffering often exposes our need for God and our need to feel loved. During Visio Divina, when we are able to be open to receive Love, our humble acknowledgment of our need allows the love of God to be poured into our hearts through the Spirit. Suffering therefore produces hope. The hope that does not disappoint is found in an experienced love relationship with God, who desires the opportunity to pour out the Spirit into our hearts, producing a hope that does not disappoint.

Suffering has been a significant part of many people's lives for a long time. It may seem like the suffering is never going to go away. It is in the midst of suffering when we need to experience love the most. It's my prayer that we will experience love in tangible ways as we make our way through suffering toward hope.

## *What do you think?*

1. How does your story connect with Alan's story?

2. Which part of Alan's story triggered the strongest feelings in you?

3. What questions do you have?

# NINE

# Fear

*If perfect love overcomes fear,
why am I still afraid?*

When Beth was born, her mother was struggling to believe she was loved. Her insecurity resulted in her need to appear perfect. One aspect of her struggle with perfectionism was a battle with food and her refusal to gain weight. While her mind told her she wasn't thin enough, her heart told her she wasn't worth loving. Unfortunately for Beth, she grew up doubting whether she was worth loving, which accompanied the voices of her mother's demand of perfection. Beth and I met once a week for spiritual direction for approximately eight months, during which she wrote the following.

After a few minutes of Visio Divina, God told me to put my hand on my heart and he would lead me in the process of healing. I experienced God taking me deep into my own heart. He said, "I have done a good work here." God showed me the layers of my heart as he took me through the places that he has touched. I saw most of my heart: all of the places were white and pure. Then we got to the bottom of my heart and there was a place of darkness. I asked God what that was. I heard God say, "This is the place that I will set free today." God then showed me an image that I was familiar with; my little girl was trapped in a cage. It was a cage not inside prison walls, but outside in an open space. Solid at the top and the bottom, there were bars all around the sides. My little girl was looking through the bars at me as an adult woman. God invited me to talk with her. She told me she was lonely in the cage and she wanted to come and be with me. I asked God to make that happen. God told me I needed to be the one to invite her to come out of the cage, because I had put her there in the first place.

I hear Karen praying for me. She is praying that God's perfect love would remove all fear. I hear her asking God to remove any fear that is contributing to me not being able to go and be with my little girl. I feel a release of something that wants to choke me as it leaves. The presence of God's love seems to have set me free from a demonic spirit of fear.

There had been several previous experiences in my healing journey in which God has shown me an image of a little girl in a cage. During most of these times I felt afraid and powerless to do anything to change her circumstances. At an earlier time, four years ago, I recorded in my journal the following words I heard God speak to my heart: "Little Elizabeth contains the root of your fear of loneliness and abandonment.... Little Elizabeth has been abandoned by you, and you now fear that same painful abandonment happening to you, in your intimate relationships."

During this Visio Divina experience, I walked up to the cage with a deep love in my heart for the little girl and knew I wanted her to be free from being lonely, inside the cage. I opened the door, told her I loved her and that I was sorry my choices had encaged her. I invited her to come out and be with me and with God. God invited me to embrace the little girl. I remember feeling afraid because I knew she was angry with me. As I held her, we wept together and she thanked me for wanting her. During this encounter, Jesus was standing beside me, looking down and smiling. He knew that he couldn't do this work without my choice to embrace a forsaken part of me. And I knew that I couldn't make that choice without his presence beside me.

Jesus, then, reached down and picked us both up, one of us in each of his arms. He held us close to his chest. I heard Jesus say, "From this day forth, you shall be one. The caged part of you has been set free. You belong to yourself and you also belong to me."

Jesus, then, turned and looked at the cage. He outstretched his hand and the power that went forth from his hand immediately consumed the cage. I watched it disappear in an instant. What had once been was no more. And I knew that my life would never be the same. For the first time in my life, my adult self was present with this little child part of me.

In my current Visio Divina, God showed me my heart once again. The part of my heart at the bottom, that was previously dark, had been made white. I had been healed. I heard God say to me, "This day you have been healed and set free. You will never be encaged again."

The cage to me represented the "respectability" of my family especially as it came through my mother. The need to uphold the image of respectability encaged the true core of who I was as a child. The cage also represents the restrictions that I put upon myself to become someone that I wasn't. As I child, I was very uninhibited with my emotions and my speech. I learned over time, through my mother, to edit out, suppress, and restrict the expression of certain parts of me. In doing so, I encaged the child. The child is the expressive creative, uninhibited, vibrant, core of my being.

I feel more integrated with my self, the child and the adult. I am more integrated in my heart, which to me is my core passion, dreams, and uninhibited expression of the deepest parts of me, the creative side of me. The part of me that is not fearful. That part of me has become more integrated with the adult side of me that represents my mind, my intellect, and my adult choices. I now feel more integrated at the core of who I am. There is much less of a split of my expression of the heart and the mind of who I am.

This experience with God is a continuation of a long journey of healing of the deep places of loneliness and abandonment within my soul. I originally thought that healing of "loneliness" would come through my connection with God or my connection with others. While these are important parts of my healing journey, this experience in Visio Divina highlights a significant part of my healing came when God helped to unite the child and adult part of me through freeing the child from the cage within which she had been bound. I don't struggle as much with deep feelings of loneliness and abandonment. One of the

things I have experienced since this healing is a greater
desire to be creative, expressive, and spontaneous.

Reflecting on the words of Isaiah can help us understand
Elizabeth's experience.

> *But this is a people robbed and plundered, all of them are*
> *trapped in holes and hidden in prisons; they have become*
> *a prey with no one to rescue, a spoil with no one to say,*
> *"Restore!"*                                    —Isaiah 42:22

> *I have kept you and given you as a covenant to the people, to*
> *establish the land, to apportion the desolate heritages; saying*
> *to the prisoners, "Come out," to those who are in darkness,*
> *"Show yourselves."*                          —Isaiah 49:8b–9a

The words of the prophet Isaiah of Babylon resound
in the people of Israel's ears. "Restore" (Isaiah 42:22),
"Come out" (Isaiah 49:9), "Show yourselves" (Isaiah
49:9). The people are in exile in Babylon and are described by the writer as being "trapped in holes" and
"hidden in prisons." Yahweh sends the prophet to speak
words of comfort that God is on their side and desires
to free them from their captivity. The biblical metaphors
of being trapped in holes and hidden in prisons can be
understood as descriptors of their need for inner trans-

formation in addition to their need for freedom from the oppressive Babylonian government and physical restoration to their land. Yahweh sends the servant, a prophet, to offer hope and bring healing to these people who have no hope.

Elizabeth experienced Yahweh speaking words to her that offered freedom from her internal cage of "respectability" that had trapped a vibrant core of her being. Her experience of God dissolving the cage contributed to her feeling more integrated with the little girl who contained her creative, spontaneous, and expressive personality. God freed this little girl as the adult Elizabeth cooperated with the Spirit, choosing to accept and embrace this exiled part of her soul. Indeed, this exiled little girl was restored to where she belonged, united with Elizabeth's conscious self. The little girl who felt hopeless in her cage was now home.

Reflecting on one of the writings of John can help us understand another aspect of Elizabeth's Visio Divina.

> *There is no fear in love, but perfect love casts out fear; for fear has to do with punishment. . . .* — 1 John 4:18

Beth grew up fearing that she would be punished if she didn't behave in such a way that was "respectable." She longed to be more creative, expressive, and spontaneous, but this part of her soul was caged by fear, the fear of being punished when she did something wrong. As she connected to this fearful part of her soul, God showed her how to love the caged little girl. As she began to love herself, the power of perfect love embodied in Jesus dissolved her cage and freed her from something she described as wanting to choke her as it leaves. The presence of darkness cannot remain in the presence of light. The presence of fear, in this case, a demonic spirit, could not remain in the presence of love. The spirit of fear that contributed to Beth's fear of facing her own experience of abandonment and rejection was overcome by the presence of something greater and more powerful, the presence of Love. The power of Jesus' ultimate act of love, his death on the cross, and resurrection overcame all powers, including the demonic. As little Elizabeth experienced God, she experienced this power and this love overcoming fear.

## *What do you think?*

1. How does your story connect with Beth's story?

2. Which part of Beth's story triggered the strongest feelings in you?

3. Can you identify with a part of you feeling encaged?

4. How does your fear keep you trapped?

5. Will you be open to let Love come into this part of your soul?

# LOVE

## BEING LOVED AND LOVING OTHERS

Shame makes me feel separated from God: How can I be intimate? Shame makes me feel separated from others: Is there any way to let myself be vulnerable? I'm angry with God: Is that okay? How can I learn to serve others without hurting myself? How can I live sacrificially without being a doormat? I address these questions in the following chapters as I share stories of people who have been loved through Visio Divina. A central component of Visio Divina is the experience of God's love, which can help us better love ourselves and, therefore, help us better love others.

# TEN

# OVERCOMING ∫HAME

*Shame makes me feel separated from God —
How can I be intimate?*

Laura was twenty-eight years old at the time of the following experience of Visio Divina. It was one of many experiences with God that contributed to her healing. Her journey with me as her spiritual director consisted of weekly sessions lasting over six months. Laura's parents divorced when she was eight years old, and as a result her mother was a single parent when she raised her. Laura initially sought spiritual direction to try to overcome some of the areas in her personal life where she felt stuck. After learning of Laura's family background, her experiences of emotional disconnection with her parents, her current struggles with behavior she could not change that made her want to hide in shame, and her inability to feel that God loved and accepted her in the

midst of those choices, I invited God to help her understand some of the deeper issues that contributed to her
feelings of failure in her ability to love and accept herself.
Laura tells the following story.

As we (Karen and I) sat in silence, I began to sense an
image coming into my mind. I see a picture of a place, and
in the distance I see Jesus sitting on a big stone by a river:
a clear river that makes no sound. I am hiding behind a
tree and peeking out, watching Jesus from where I am.
He is sitting on the rock with his back to me. But then he
turns and starts to walk towards me. I am so afraid. I am
panic-stricken; my stomach is in knots, and my hands
are cold and clammy from fear. I am so afraid that I peek
out from behind the tree to see where he has reached.
I keep peeking out from behind the tree for fear that he
will see me. I peek and then quickly come back behind
the tree.

The closer he gets, the more I am afraid. The closer
he comes, the stiffer I become. Now I can't even look
from behind the tree. I am very stiff and very afraid. I feel
crippled and paralyzed with fear. But then, he stops. He
is not far away from me. I watch him come towards me.
He stretches out his hand towards me, but I am still so

afraid. I don't want to come out, because I am ashamed and afraid.

"What if he finds out?"

Jesus does not move. But his eyes are very transparent, and the love I see in them is what brings the release I need. I am still afraid, but I know he loves me. He comes closer, and I allow him to draw me from behind the tree.

As Laura described what she was experiencing, seeing Jesus on the rock and then walking toward her, I sensed a prompting from the Spirit that God wanted to love her in such a way that would begin to free her from layers of shame that were impeding her ability to feel loved by God. I heard Laura say in a timid, fearful voice, "What if he finds out?" While God was walking toward her she hid behind the tree. So, I asked Laura to look into his eyes and tell me what she saw. "His eyes are filled with love and compassion. Oh, he loves me."

As Laura was being encountered by God, I sensed the Spirit was prompting me to pray for God's love to envelop her and release her from shame. I saw, with the eyes of my heart, an image of God freeing her from what looked like a dark blanket of the shame that covered her soul. Through God's love Laura was free from this blanket of

shame and began to feel lightness and increased freedom
to enter into intimacy with God.

The theme of Laura's story is similar to another part
of the story of Adam and Eve in the Garden of Eden. In
this scene of the biblical story,

> *They heard the sound of the Lord God walking in the garden*
> *at the time of the evening breeze, and the man and his wife*
> *hid themselves from the presence of the Lord God among the*
> *trees of the garden. But the Lord God called to the man, and*
> *said to him, "Where are you?" He said, "I heard the sound*
> *of you in the garden, and I was afraid, because I was naked;*
> *I hid myself." He said, "Who told you that you were naked?*
> *Have you eaten from the tree of which I commanded you*
> *not to eat?"*                              — Genesis 3:8–11

Just as Laura did in her Visio Divina, Adam and Eve
hide behind a tree, and yet the Lord God talked with
these two naked ashamed people, asking them a question that can only be understood in light of that earlier
part of the story where they eat from a forbidden tree.
However, with Laura, I wasn't sure what behavior she
was struggling with and what she feared God finding
out. Apparently she was doing something she believed
God told her not to do. Although we really don't know
what the tree in the garden actually signifies, an important part of the story is that God told Adam and Eve not

to eat it. After consuming its fruit, they hid, were fearful and ashamed.

In the midst of experiencing God's presence after doing the very thing God told them not to do, God asks a question that God still asks each one of us today, "Where are you?" It's a question we all long to hear from the Source of Love we all long to experience. Even when we are hiding, when we feel the most unlovable, most of us want to be found by someone who can love us. Adam and Eve believed they did something wrong. Most of us hide when we are bad. We fear punishment and rejection, and shame begins to cover our soul. We ask our own questions: how could God still love me when I am so bad? In the deepest places within our soul we hide, fearing that the worst will happen to us, that we will be rejected and our biggest fear will be confirmed; we aren't loved.

Some of us have been hiding since we lived in our mother's womb. Feeling rejected and having emotions of not being wanted is actually experienced by the developing fetus and can contribute to adult struggles of feeling unloved and rejected. Those feelings go unhealed until we experience a love that finds us in our place of hiding, gradually helps us overcome our fears, begins to heal our feelings of rejection and unlovability, and ultimately loves

us into being. As we are loved, we begin to feel the freedom to come alive, becoming the person we were created
to be, who we really are.

An important part of the biblical story is that God is
shown not only as a distant all-powerful creator of the
universe, but as one who is intimate with us as children.
God walks and talks with Adam and Eve and chooses
to be close to his creation. In his subtle way, the writer
of the story highlights how important it is to know God
in this way by how he refers to God. Gordon Wenham,
an Old Testament scholar, provides insight that helps me
understand the significance of how the writer describes
God. The term "the Lord God" is used by the narra-
tor in chapters 2–3 as the primary way to characterize
God, and it isn't used anywhere else in the Old Testament. Usually one word or the other is used, but here
the two are combined, suggesting that this story reveals
both God's character as sovereign creator of the universe
(God) and his intimate covenant-like relationship with
humankind (Yahweh, the Lord). The term "Lord God" is
used 20 times in the garden story. The only time the term
"God" is used, describing God as a distant all-powerful
creator, is in the interaction with the serpent. In essence,
the serpent used the term to describe God as only the
distant all-powerful creator, rather then using the term

that describes God as both intimate covenant-like friend *and* all-powerful creator.

In order to reestablish trust with Adam and Eve, the "Lord God" appears as an intimate, covenantal friend who walks and talks with his children. The serpent would like for us to believe that "God" is only a distant all-powerful creator. The "Lord God," however, wants us to know that he can find us when we are hiding, loves us in the midst of our choices, and can reestablish a relationship of trust. Our shame doesn't have to separate us from him. The Lord God knows you are hiding. The Lord God is asking, "Where are you?"

Many of us have been taught that God banished Adam and Eve from the garden because of their sin, a theology that results in our fearing God's punishment rather than experiencing God in the midst of our choices that reveal our inability to love. If God kicks us out of the garden when we are bad, then it makes sense that we should hide. But, if the Lord God pursues us in the midst of our shame, knowing we are hiding not because of something he has done but because of our human tendency to personalize our bad-ness, then we can open ourselves to receive the love we long for and need, knowing that our relationship with the Lord God is secure. The Lord God will never leave us nor forsake us.

Shame serves as a barrier between ourselves, and others. This barrier can prevent us from experiencing intimacy with God, ourselves and others. What we need most in the midst of our shame is to be pursued and loved in such a way that the shame melts away. The difficulty is that shame contributes to hiding, and when we hide, it is hard to be found. Visio Divina helps create space for God to find us in our shame. As we experience God's presence of love, we can begin to be released from our shame so we can begin to stop hiding and begin to experience intimacy with God, ourselves, and others.

## *What do you think?*

1. How does your story connect with Laura's story?

2. Which part of Laura's story triggered the strongest feelings in you?

3. Is there any part of story of the Garden of Eden that surprises you?

4. How are you hiding from God?

5. Will you let God find you?

# ELEVEN

# VULNERABILITY

*Shame makes me feel separated from others —*
*Is there any way to let myself be vulnerable?*

Previously I shared how empty and unloved I felt after completing a successful conference for women in athletics and recounted how I was learning how to love by learning how to sit with God, learning how to let God's love meet my deepest longings. It took a long time to know God in such a way that I could begin to experience intimacy with God and others. One reason why it took so long is because I struggled with shame that kept me at a distance from the people I was serving and even from the people who wanted to know me well. I was comfortable when I was up front teaching, alone writing, or envisioning some new idea or project. Interacting intimately with other people, making myself vulnerable, was much less comfortable and was an experience I often avoided.

Shame serves to protect us from being seen and ultimately shields us from being hurt by providing a layer
that covers our vulnerability and pain. If we aren't seen,
we cannot be hurt. Shame, therefore, helps us from being
hurt again. Unfortunately, it also prevents us from feeling
loved and experiencing intimacy. When we hide behind
shame, to protect ourselves, we can't experience life to
the fullest, life in relationships with others whom we love
and by whom we are loved.

Adam and Eve hid behind their shame in the garden.
God pursued them and covered them with clothes, re-
moving the garment of shame they didn't need to wear.
God encountering them in love replaced the shame with
clothing that enabled them to go on living in the garden.
We need to be encountered by love in the midst of our
shame so that we can come out from the places we are
hiding and let ourselves be vulnerable so we can live life
more fully in the garden as God intended.

The process of being free from the shame that contributed to my hiding was my ongoing experience of
being encountered by love. Much of my healing journey included being encountered by God and others who
loved me in the midst of my shame. When we are hiding
we need to be found. When we are found we need to
be loved.

My feeling unloved as a little girl resulted in my thinking that I was unlovable. My shame covered me and protected me from experiencing what I thought was reality: that if people really knew me, they wouldn't love me. I needed something that could correct my false reality and begin to show me that I am lovable. My journey consisted of experiencing God this way. Others experience a spouse, a partner, a therapist, a community, a spiritual director, or a friend helping them experience the reality that they are lovable. My experience was that God could get in to the places where I was hiding and could get close enough to envelop my shame so that I could begin to feel loved.

10:15 a.m., the school bell rang. It was finally time for recess. The two hours between the first bell signaling the start of the new school day and the second bell can seem like a long time for most first graders. On this day, those two hours felt like an eternity for me as a six-year-old girl.

As usual, Mrs. Gossage dismissed her students to the playground for their fifteen-minute break. This day she dismissed them without allowing them to go to the classroom closet to check out their favorite playground toy. I am sure the children thought it strange, and much grumbling was heard, but eventually I could also hear the quiet which surfaced following the last pitter-patter sounds of footsteps moving quickly past the classroom closet and out the door.

Mrs. Gossage, knowingly, made her way across the classroom to the closet that was in view from her desk, yet was hidden behind a wall, out of sight from any of the student desks. With one hand she turned the knob and opened the door. With her other hand, she reached into the dark corner of the closet, inviting me, a frightened six-year-old little girl, out of my place of hiding.

It was always a bit hectic in the morning as the family got ready for school and work. The process of getting five children, ages six to seventeen, out the door and into the car was often interrupted by some minor disaster — a shoelace broken, homework forgotten, the alarm clock refusing to sound. For me, the youngest child, it wasn't often an external disaster that slowed the process, it was usually something of an internal crisis that made the morning routine so difficult. I was a very timid little girl. I was often found cowering behind the back of my mom's jacket. I cried regularly. I spoke rarely.

On this day, I was petrified of being seen. Mom dropped me off at the school at 8:30 a.m., fifteen minutes late for class. The thought of walking into the classroom and having all the students look at me was frightening, so much so that I decided to prevent it from happening. I stepped into the classroom and immediately slipped into the closet located just inside the front door. There I sat, in the dark, for nearly two hours, fearful that I would be found out.

Years later, in 1995, I enrolled as a seminary student. As I've already mentioned, I had just organized a successful ministry event, completed a master's degree in counseling, and had spent three years working with college students in Arizona. I hadn't intended to study in seminary, which required I take a break from ministry Instead, I intended to continue to go to the hurting people "out there," especially women, who needed to be loved. Instead, God came to me, a hurting, vulnerable woman who needed to be loved. Me, hurting? Me, vulnerable? From my perspective, my understanding of reality at that time, the words "hurting" and "vulnerable" did not apply to me. Instead, the words, "successful," "capable," "competent," and "independent" were adjectives that were much easier to embrace as descriptions of myself.

However, when God put his hand on the doorknob to all my closets and began to invite me to come out into the light, I began to see myself the way God sees me. The paradox seems to be that you don't really know you're hiding in shame until you are found. You see, the little girl that I was who hid in the closet many years ago,

fearful of really being seen by my peers and by myself, re-
mained a timid little girl, covered with shame, for most of
my life. The closets just changed form. Academic accom-
plishment, image, athletic success, relationships, ministry
success, spiritual gifting — all make good closets. But
God saw through those closets and reached in, over a
period of years, and gently, lovingly, and powerfully enabled me to see why I was hiding. With one hand of love
God opened the door of the closet in my heart and revealed to me a place of pain that had been hidden for
many years. With the other hand of love God took my
hand and invited me to enter into the pain and agony of
this experience.

To learn that I was fearful of dying as a little girl because I never felt the security of an emotional bond with
my mother was one of a number of very painful vulner-
abilities I needed to confront in myself. As I grieved the
loss of the relationship I did not have with my mom, a part
of me truly felt as if I had died. At other times, the intense
pain I felt meant I was still alive, so that somehow to feel
the pain was actually a life-giving experience. The shame
that covered my soul was there, in my deep unconscious,
because of my mother's inability to bond to me, in turn,
because of her mother's inability to bond to her, and back
farther because of *her* mother's inability to bond to *her*; so

that, all of us, generation after generation, felt unloved. Although she had every intention and desire to give me the love I needed, my mother's limited capacity to love me left me, as an infant, fearing that I would die if she left my side. I never felt the security of a love that enabled me to know I would go on living even if we were separated. My fear of death, therefore, was rooted in my feeling that she would die and there would be nothing left in me to enable me to live. This internalized sense of radical vulnerability and shame covered my soul from infancy.[1] In light of my mother's unconscious limited ability to emotionally connect with me, I protected myself by shutting down, began to believe I was unlovable, and soon clothed myself in shame. I hid behind this covering until, much later, I began through Visio Divina to experience love in

---

1. Shame has been called an "attachment emotion" (Lewis 1980). It can result when a primary caregiver is unable to respond positively to an infant's longing to be loved, and therefore the infant is unable to experience a secure emotional bond. The primary caregiver can spontaneously and unconsciously block the infant's attempt to attach, which can result in the infant experiencing shame. This experience can disrupt what Winnicott (1958) called the child's need for "going-on-being." For more information on shame written by experts in the fields of psychoanalysis and neurobiology, see Winnicott (1958), Siegel (1999), and Schore (2003a, 2003b). For further reading in easy to understand language to help you learn more about how your early attachment history influences the way you love, feel, and act, see Clinton and Sibcy (2002).

the place within my soul that felt dead. God began to comfort and love me back to life.

In one Visio Divina, all I could see was darkness. There was no image. There was no light. Pain was all there was, the pain of being disconnected from a source of love and life. Then, gradually, there was a voice who said, "I'm here." I recognized that voice because I had heard it hundreds of times before, a voice of comfort, peace, and penetrating insight. "I love you." It is still dark. There are still no images. But I feel peace. My God is here, and my God loves me. Then the image comes.... It's me; I'm an infant, and I'm crying. My mom comes quickly in response to my cry and picks me up. I stop crying. She puts me down and walks away. I see the baby close her eyes, and then I see a dark blanket cover her body. She lies there with the dark blanket covering her. She doesn't cry, but she doesn't seem content. Then I see Jesus walk into the room. He picks up the baby and says, "I'm here. I love you." I feel a heaviness lift off my body and begin to feel my chest open. There is warmth in my chest as Jesus holds me close to him. I can feel love entering my body. It feels calm and strong. I can begin to let myself go into this love. As I sink in, I feel comforted and filled. I feel like I am coming alive on the inside; a part of me that I've never felt before is alive. The blanket of shame is gone. I am beginning to feel loved by a source of love who can give me what I need. The Source will be there over and over again as I continue to experience the healing of this fragile place within my soul.

As I felt my vulnerable infant self longing for love, another Visio Divina showed me that instead of shame protecting this fragile place part of my soul, God was, in fact, doing it for me.

I saw an image of a thin, weak, fragile candle, with a small smoldering flame. I then saw hands, God's hands, cupped around this flame, protecting it from being blown out. I also saw an image of a strong, thick, solid candle with a flickering flame. The strength and size of the base of the candle seemed that it would enable the flame to burn indefinitely.

The flame of my smoldering wick was growing in strength. The fragile place that was longing to feel more alive was beginning to be protected by something other than shame. The reality of God's love was enabling me to let go of a shame that had been protecting me from getting hurt again. Once again, the prophet Isaiah helps me understand my Visio Divina.

> A bruised reed he will not break, and a smoldering wick he will not snuff out.                    — Isaiah 42:3

As I felt protected by God's love, I was able to begin to take more risks in loving others. As I made myself more vulnerable and took more risks in loving others, I began to experience intimacy, the place where we experience mutuality of feeling known and loved.

## *What do you think?*

1. How does your story connect with my story?

2. Which part of my story triggered the strongest feelings in you?

3. Take a few moments to enter in to a place of rest where God can help you be more vulnerable and can love you in your shame.

If you have been practicing Visio Divina on your own (see page 42 for a reminder of how to do it), ask God to take you to a place within your soul where God wants to love you. If the emotions feel too powerful or overwhelming, or you feel stuck, please begin to meet with a spiritual director or psychotherapist who can help you experience love in the place of your vulnerability and shame.

# TWELVE

# Anger

*I'm angry with God —*
*Is that okay?*

Leticia's husband had an affair. After discovering that he had cheated on her, she chose to forgive him in hopes that her marriage could be saved. Her anger was being expressed in requiring that he come home immediately after work and tell her exactly what he did when he wasn't at home or at work. She didn't give him the freedom to go out on his own, and she required him to stay home even when his male friends were playing poker. Leticia came to spiritual direction because she felt God was absent. She talked about hearing God's voice and experiencing God's love prior to her husband's affair, but since then, God didn't seem to care. She went to church but had recently stopped singing in the choir.

After getting to know Leticia a little bit better, I introduced her to Visio Divina. Since she had heard God's

voice in the past, she was open to giving it a try, but didn't
expect much. As we sat together in silence, I gently asked
God to take her to a place within her soul where she most
needed to be loved. For a long time she was quiet. I didn't
think anything was happening. Five minutes later, without much emotion, she said, "I hate him." We sat together
quietly for a few more minutes, and then I heard her say,
with a bit more emotion, "I want to kill him," and she
described what she was experiencing.

> I see a time when Eric came home with flowers in his
> hands. He said he worked late that night and wanted to
> show me how much he loved me.
>
> I see another time when Eric bought me a ring that I
> really loved. He said he was sorry that he was working
> so many extra hours, but he was happy to be making
> extra money to afford to buy special things that I really
> wanted.
>
> Now, I see the time I answered an incoming call on
> his cell phone. The bitch was on the other end. I picked
> it up and she said, "Hi, Honey."
>
> I hate him and I want to kill him.
>
> Then she was silent.

At this point, I wasn't sure who she was angry at, God
or Eric. I asked if it would be okay if God were with

her in these places of pain. She nodded her head up and down, yes. So I said, "God, where are you?" Without emotion she began to share with me that she saw God in the room with her when she picked up the cell phone. God was sitting on the couch, watching. Then she said, "Why didn't you do anything to stop him? You could have stopped him!" A few seconds later, she quietly said, "He is walking toward me. He is standing right in front of me. I want to hit him. He says it's okay if I hit him. I see myself hitting his chest. He says, 'Tell me more how you feel.' I hate him, and I hate you for letting it happen." At this point, Leticia burst into tears, feeling the pain. She cried intense tears of sadness and hurt and then slowly grew quiet. After a few minutes, she said, "I hear him saying it is okay to feel the pain." And she continued to cry.

Sometimes our anger is an expression of pain. If we don't express the anger, we don't get to be freed from the hurt, and the anger comes out in some other way. In Leticia's case, her anger it was expressed by controlling and punishing her husband. Leticia had a choice to continue to control and punish her husband or to get in touch with the anger and let the anger take her to the pain. Then she could feel it, grieve it, and gradually begin to forgive.

A glimpse into scripture shows us a similar principle.

> *Why aren't you doing anything?*
> *Are you sleeping?*
> *Will you rouse yourself and do something?*
> *I am trapped here on the ground and I can't get up!*

Have you ever said words like that to God? If so, you are in good company. God's chosen servant David complains about what seems to be God's absence at a time when he really needs God's help. These lines from Psalm 44 record the great King David expressing his anger toward God. He seems to be fed up, tired of waiting for God to answer. He is no longer patiently praising God for God's goodness. He speaks honestly and expresses his anger and his disappointment.

God's response, in Psalm 45,[1] reveals God's compassion toward David. Instead of punishing him for being angry, God reminds him who he is:

> *You are the most handsome of men;*
> *grace is poured upon your lips;*
> *therefore God has blessed you forever.*
> *Gird your sword on your thigh, O mighty one,*
> *in your glory and majesty.*
> *In your majesty ride on victoriously*
> *for the cause of truth and to defend the right;*
> *let your right hand teach you dread deeds.*

1. Old Testament scholar David C. Mitchell (1997) provides an insightful perspective on why Psalm 45 is a response to Psalm 44.

> *Your arrows are sharp*
> *in the heart of the king's enemies;*
> *the peoples fall under you.*

So God seems to be okay with David's anger. God responds to David's cry of frustration and desperation. That fact that God responds shows us that God can handle our anger. God isn't weak and fragile; God is strong and can hold us, even in the midst of our rage. God stays present with David, and after David screams at God, God responds by speaking to him about who he is. The fact that God stays present and then speaks shows us that God is neither angry with our anger nor disappointed when we aren't able to trust. God responds by speaking to a deep fear within David's heart. David is a leader who is on the ground after his enemies have not succumbed in battle. The victory has not yet been won. A leader is questioning his ability to lead, and the people are questioning whether God has abandoned them. In the midst of a battle which he seems to be losing, his anger and desperation reflects deep places of insecurity and the emotional pain caused by this fragile place within David.

God knew why David was angry. God held David's anger and then responded in love. Anger is an authentic human emotion that God gave us. Being angry is a part of being human. What we do with our anger is a part of learning how to love. We either express it in ways that are safe to ourselves and others, or we use it to hurt, control, manipulate, dominate, or punish others or ourselves. A more loving way to deal with our anger, though, is to get in touch with it and express it in healthy ways. During Visio Divina, our anger can be expressed directly at God. As God did with David, God will do with us: God contains our anger and then loves us in the place where we need it most. If you are angry with God, it's okay. Let God know.

## *What do you think?*

1. How does your story connect with David's story?

2. Which part of David's story triggered the strongest feelings in you?

3. Leticia expressed her anger by controlling and punishing. Are you doing that?

4. Are you ready to express your anger in healthy ways?

5. One way to begin to express your anger is to write an honest letter to the person you are angry at. You won't ever give the person this letter. If you feel

angry at God, write a letter honestly expressing your emotions.

6. If you have been practicing Visio Divina on your own (see page 42 for a reminder of how to do it), ask God to take you to a place within your soul where God wants to love you. If the emotions feel too powerful or overwhelming, begin to meet with a spiritual director or psychotherapist who can help you express your anger and feel your pain in healthy and safe ways.

# ſERVICE

*How can I learn to serve others
without hurting myself?*

Donna came to spiritual direction in search of something. She really didn't know what it was, but she knew something was missing. She had a hunch it had to do with God, but she didn't think that God would do much to help her out. She was in a quandary. Her fifteen years of service as a social worker with abused children who had been removed from their families had taken a toll on her view of God to the point of doubting that God was real at all, or, if real, God could do anything to change the suffering in our world. She had seen too much pain, too much hopelessness, too much despair, too much agony, and too much grief, and she no longer believed that God could help any of these realities. But somewhere deep inside her was a stirring, a searching, a longing for something.

Donna didn't really like her job very much anymore, having grown to resent how much the children took from her, how they needed her so much, and the fact that so few people chose to go into the city to work among those who need love the most. She was angry at the church, angry at God, angry at her co-workers, and was struggling to believe whether any of this was worth continuing to do. She had given fifteen years of her life, and now she couldn't see any purpose or meaning in it. Donna was on the verge of burnout.

I listened to Donna's struggles. I sat with her in her anger. I tried to understand the deep feelings of resentment, and I began to hear the longings within her soul leading her to search for something more. She shared with me how she felt discouraged that so few people were being helped by her care. In fact, there was a specific little girl we often talked about. Donna was especially drawn to this little girl who had been abused by her father and then sent off to a Catholic boarding school to be raised by the sisters and the priest. Donna could identify strongly with the angst and anger this little girl had toward God. If God loved her so much, like the priest and sisters told her, why did God allow the abuse to happen, and why did she, who did nothing wrong, have to be taken out of her family's home to live in an environment she didn't like?

As we continued to talk, I learned about Donna's child-hood. Her father had abused her when she was four. He was a pastor and preached every Sunday morning about the love of God, and then when he came home he must have forgotten about that love because what he did to Donna in no way reflected the love of a father. As Donna began to share this abuse with me, she began to make some connections between her commitment to work in the inner city among children who had been abused and her own longing to see her little girl, the four-year-old who lived inside of her, rescued from the abusive situation she endured.

Donna and I talked more about the little girl she got to know through her work in the inner city. We talked about the sensitivity of her spirit, yet the honesty of her anger and rage. We talked about how this little girl was creative, yet most of her artwork expressed the pain and anguish of the abuse. Donna was especially struck by the fact that this little girl continued to go to church. She woke up in the morning on her own, got dressed, made her own breakfast, and walked to the little Catho-lic church down the street. Donna expressed amazement at the fact that this little girl wanted to continue to go to church even while she struggled, wondering how God could really love her. But every morning, she got up and she went to church. Eventually I learned that Donna actually envied this little girl, because in the midst of her pain and questioning, she went to a place that Donna hated but secretly longed to enjoy again.

Donna and I continued to talk. As the feelings of abuse came to the surface, I suggested she meet with a therapist in addition to our work together in spiritual direction. Donna agreed, and she eventually began to meet with a counselor who helped her work through the pain of her abuse. When I introduced Donna to Visio Divina, she immediately said "yes," remembering as a little girl how much she liked to pray. When I asked her about those memories, she shared with me that she felt close to God when she was a little girl, that she liked to talk to him, and she thought He actually talked back sometimes.

So, together, we began to do Visio Divina. Donna had images of God being with her. The first image was of a little girl sitting on a swing. When I asked her if she had a sense of where God was, she said, "I see Jesus coming to sit next to me on the swing. He has his swing. I have my swing. We are just swinging together." When I asked her how that felt, she said "It feels good. It's okay that he has his own swing and I have my own swing." In subsequent sessions, we continued to do Visio Divina together. God continues to swing with her until one day Donna heard

God's voice tell her that he loved her. She had a hard time believing this at first and thought she had made it up. When I asked her if she thought this was something she might make up, she laughed and said, "No way. I don't think God loves me."

In this way, God began to earn the trust of the little girl who had a hard time trusting men. With time, Donna began to experience Jesus coming closer to her. During one Visio Divina Donna shared that she saw Jesus standing in front of the little girl on the swing, inviting her to come off the swing and to hold his hand. Donna hesitantly said yes to this invitation and then she shared the following.

> I'm holding Jesus' hand. He and I are walking to a bench. He sits down on the bench and he is inviting me to sit next to him. I think it is okay to sit next to him. I think he feels safe. Jesus and I are now sitting on the bench. I am still holding his hand. It feels good to hold his hand. It feels good just to sit here with Jesus.

So, for the next few months, during Visio Divina, Jesus sat with Donna on that bench, and the little girl longing to be loved and cared for began to trust him, to feel loved.

It took a while for Donna to move from a place of burnout to a place of well-being. Part of her process was learning that she was trying to meet the needs of her little abused girl by trying to take care of the needs of the abused children in the city, so that when she realized the little girl part of her that was longing to be loved, she made space and time to love this little girl. She began to go on personal retreats. She continued to meet with a therapist, and as she entered into the process of her own healing, she began to feel less anger at God and more hope that she would one day find meaning and purpose.

Sometimes we can hurt ourselves as we serve others. When feelings of resentment and anger come to the surface as we serve others, we can understand these feelings as possible signs that there is a place within us that feels neglected and unloved. Often, we meet the needs of others without being aware of our own needs that are trying to be met in the service of others. When we do this, we actually are using others for the purpose of our own unmet needs. Part of the process of learning how to love others is becoming self aware of our own needs and our tendency to misdirect our longing for love in the service of others. When our unmet needs and longings for love are the primary motivations for serving others, we not only can feel disappointed that our service doesn't

meet our deepest longings for intimacy and love, we self-
ishly use others our in our attempts to meet those needs.
Learning how to love ourselves can enable us to learn
how to serve others without hurting ourselves.

## *What do you think?*

1. How does your story connect with Donna's story?

2. Which part of Donna's story triggered the strongest
   feelings in you?

3. If you are feeling on the edge of burnout, please
   begin to talk with someone about your frustration
   and anger. If possible, begin to meet with a person
   who can help you understand the deeper motives of
   your heart in terms of unmet longings for love that
   contribute to your feelings of burnout.

# FOURTEEN

# ⨍ACRIFICE

*How can I learn to live sacrificially
without being a doormat?*

Doormats get walked on. Usually at a doorway, people step on them as they go into a house or building. Doormats aren't usually recognized, aren't often appreciated, and are often taken for granted. Who wants to be a doormat?

Robert came to spiritual direction seeking to understand God better. He was on a journey, one that included exploring different faiths in hopes that he would find God and experience more meaning in his life. A math teacher working with 7th graders in a local junior high school, he chose his career as a teacher thinking that he would find meaning in educating and mentoring junior high kids. After teaching for four years, he enjoyed some parts of the job, yet other aspects of his work he found overwhelming. The needs of the kids who came from such broken homes contributed to his feeling like he was a father more than a teacher. The pain of the kids, especially as they talked about their home life, was something that Robert had a hard time leaving at school when he went home at the end of the day. He often worried about his kids and gave extra time after school in mentoring and just being there for them. Robert had a girlfriend, but she recently broke up with him because he wasn't there for her enough. He didn't understand why she left him. He thought he was doing the right thing in sacrificing his time and talent for the purpose of encouraging these kids. He felt sad that his girlfriend had left him, and he felt disillusioned with the whole idea of giving of himself to help others.

During one session, Robert shared with me how one of the most troubled boys from his reading group called him at midnight the night before. Robert got up and went to the boy's house to be there for him in his time of need. When I asked Robert how many times that happened, he said it usually happened three or four times a week. He also began to share how he didn't feel appreciated by the kids for all that he was sacrificing, getting up in the middle of the night to be there for them, staying after school to mentor them. He didn't feel like they recognized all that he had given and all that he had sacrificed to be there for them. Basically, Robert was feeling like a doormat.

As I got to know Robert a little bit better, I learned that his father had left home when Robert was three, divorcing his mom because he had been offered a better job in another part of the country and his wife refused to relocate. Yet another time, Robert's father didn't want to give up the offer in order to stay at home with his son and be a husband to his wife. The loss of his father had an enormous impact on him, and he resolved that he was never going to live his life the way his dad lived his. He vowed never to let his work become more important than his family, but he also wanted to choose a career that gave him meaning in helping out others.

When I saw him for spiritual direction, though, Robert wasn't experiencing meaning, and, in fact, he had become like his father, sacrificing his time, energy, and talents for his job while neglecting his girlfriend and his own personal needs. When we began to explore childhood memories through Visio Divina, Robert began to experience God coming to him in such a way that began to meet his deepest longings: to feel loved and secure in the strong embrace of a father's arms. In this strong embrace, Robert felt his inner strength, and in the love of God as father, Robert began to live more out of the essence of

who he is. He said "no" to the boys at school without
feeling guilty, while still communicating that he cared for
them. As he separated from the kids at school, he realized
he didn't have to be a doormat to find meaning in helping
and serving others.

Prior to experiencing Visio Divina, Robert sacrificed
himself in order to help the kids. After months of experiencing God through Visio Divina Robert felt loved, and
an inner strength emerged within him that enabled him
to willingly choose to offer this part of himself that was
now alive to the students who needed it. In some ways,
the three-year-old little boy living inside Robert had not
been fully alive. As he began to feel alive as a result of
feeling loved in a tangible way, the essence of his humanity, a person of compassion, was expressed in caring for
his students, and he began to find that more meaningful.

Letting people walk all over us is a misunderstand-
ing of loving sacrifice. Jesus modeled a life of sacrifice,
yet he wasn't a doormat. Jesus was fully alive, able to
willingly give of himself because the source of his loving
sacrifice was rooted in the knowledge of his father's love.
Jesus' sacrifice flowed from love. When we are a doormat, our sacrifice flows from a source in our soul that
feels unloved and, ultimately, not worthy of love. We become a doormat in hopes that we will feel loved, rather

than sacrificing from a place of *being* loved. In essence, we become doormats when we don't feel loved, while we sacrifice because we know we are loved.

In willingly choosing to give his life so that we might live, Jesus is an example of compassionate love. His death is a once-and-for-all act that enables all of us to know we are loved and included in God's family. Because his sacrifice is already accomplished, we do not need to be a doormat, sacrificing ourselves in an attempt to feel loved. Instead, we need to experience the compassionate love of God as the source of our compassionate love of others.

That's why Christ's death on the cross is such a big deal to me. Through Visio Divina, I participate in Christ's death and resurrection and experience his love so I can be fully alive and able to sacrifice for others.

Loving service to others is an expression of compassion. An aspect of being human means we are compassionate. Because God lives in all of us, the core of who we are can be found in God's essence, and at that core of God's essence is compassion. Jesus' life, death, and resurrection models a way of living in love, and his sacrifice on the cross out of love enables me to live compassionately. Other faiths likewise encourage the expression of compassion. As we recognize the fullness of our humanity, we recognize our capacity to be compassionate, and we also recognize places within us that prevent us from living compassionately. I long to see the world become a place where human beings live as human beings, fully alive and fully compassionate. I believe Christ came to help us do that. As other faiths recognize God's presence within or the human potential to live compassionately, they are exuding the essence of God and the essence of Christ.

Living compassionately doesn't mean living as a doormat. Sacrificing for the needs of others doesn't mean we kill ourselves by letting people walk all over us. In order to find our life, yes, we must lose it. In order to die to ourselves, we must have a self to die to. A doormat doesn't have a self. A doormat exists but doesn't embody a source of life that enables it to engage others and then willingly choose to give of itself for the needs of others. Living sacrificially means we are willing to give up some of the things that are important to us so that others can have what they couldn't have without our help. Living sacrificially doesn't mean giving of ourselves in such a way that we no longer exist and our needs no longer matter, nor does it mean we willingly kill ourselves in the process of offering help, hope, or compassion to others. It means we willingly give up parts of ourselves that feel alive in a way that offers our aliveness to others.

Doormats get walked on. If there are places within our soul that don't really know we are loved, we may try to feel loved by sacrificing ourselves for the needs of others. If there was a need as a child for you to sacrifice yourself in order to take care of your family, or maybe someone demanded that you give up yourself for their selfish needs (such as abuse), you may have developed a pattern of living that unconsciously sacrifices yourself, resulting in your feeling like a doormat. You may resent people who don't notice how much you do for them. You may feel tired of giving yourself without receiving any-thing in return. You may feel taken for granted, and you may feel angry about that. You don't have to continue to be a doormat. However, you must learn what contributes to your behavior in order for you to experience lasting change. Visio Divina can help as you let God reveal the unconscious motives of your heart that contribute to your sacrificing yourself in your attempt to feel loved.

## *What do you think?*

1. How does your story connect with Robert's story?

2. Which part of Robert's story triggered the strongest feelings in you?

3. Take a few moments to enter into a place of rest where God can love you.

If you have been practicing Visio Divina on your own (see page 42 for a reminder of how to do it), ask God to take you to a place within your soul that is contributing to your feeling like a doormat. See if you can experience God there. If the emotions feel too powerful or overwhelming, or you feel stuck, please begin to meet with a spiritual director or psychotherapist who can help you experience love in the place of your feeling like a doormat.

# FINAL THOUGHTS ON FAITH, HOPE, AND LOVE

This book has shared some stories of people who experienced God through Visio Divina. As God encountered us in love, our lives began to change. The changes didn't happen overnight. The experience of feeling loved, experiencing hope, and knowing God was a process that for some took many years, and for others a few months. The process is an aspect of life with God. Many of us in America engage in activities expecting that our life will quickly become more meaningful and successful. Sometimes we want to jump to results. Visio Divina isn't about a quick fix or a fast track to success and meaning. A meaningful and successful life can emerge as we experience faith, hope, and love through Visio Divina, but meaning and success are just byproducts of a life in God, and they are not guaranteed.

As I hope the preceding stories and discussions make clear, a deeper experience of faith, hope, and love is available to all of us irrespective of our socio-economic level, our gender, our sexuality, our skin color, our religious preference, or our intellectual aptitude. Faith, hope, and love can emerge out of places of profound suffering and excruciating pain. Faith, hope, and love can be found in the quiet place of rest and in learning to trust the Creator of the universe, the Lover of our soul and the Source of life.

Visio Divina is a prayer practice that offers us space to become more conscious of God's presence encountering us in tangible ways, where we experience God and the fullness of our humanity. As God encounters us in love, our brain is engaged in ways that our imagination, intuition, and analytic ability help us experience something that is real. As we enter into this place of rest, we become still, and we begin to know God. In knowing God, we begin to know ourselves. In knowing ourselves, we recognize our need for healing, and we begin to feel our longings for love, intimacy, and life.

As we practice the presence of God throughout the day, both during intentional periods of quiet and rest and in the midst of the busy-ness of our world, Visio Divina can become a lifestyle. For some, however, Visio Divina will not come easily. You may want to pursue meeting with a spiritual director or others who are trained in facilitating this prayer practice. For others, though, Visio Divina will come naturally, with little effort. You will long for quiet moments with God. You will hunger after the source of love and life, and you will experience images that reveal God and help you feel emotions of being loved. You will also have questions, and you may need guidance. Even if Visio Divina comes easily, I recommend you meet with someone who you can process your experiences and who can continue to help you grow.

God can take you into deep places within your soul through Visio Divina. As you enter into these deep places, painful emotions will come to the surface. You might feel overwhelmed by the pain. When this begins to happen, please consult a spiritual director or psychotherapist who can help you manage your emotions and make your way through the pain. It is in the place of pain and suffering that new life emerges. Let someone love you in the place of your pain. It is my hope that you will experience God and others doing that in tangible ways.

# Appendices

## *Appendix One / What's Going on When It Doesn't Seem to Work?*

Visio Divina uses the right side of our brain. The right side of our brain is the intuitive, emotional, creative, and imaginative aspect of mental functioning. The development of the right side of the brain to its maximum potential requires practice, just like using the left and more analytical side of the brain. If you haven't developed the right side of your brain you won't experience Visio Divina as easily or as quickly. One of the ways to develop the right side of your brain is to "practice the presence of God" throughout the day. When you practice the presence of God, you imagine God is with you wherever you are. As you practice God's presence, you open yourself to intuitively sensing God's presence through the Spirit. Visio Divina enables you to experience God's presence in a way that enables you to utilize the right side of the brain. A result of Visio Divina is that you will become more integrated in using both the analytical and the intuitive sides of your brain.

In addition, there are times when Visio Divina is difficult because of painful and traumatic early childhood experiences that have caused a person to be disconnected from his or her heart and emotions. If it is difficult to experience Visio Divina on your own, you can meet with a person who can help you begin to understand the blocks that interfere with your experience of God in your emotions, imagination, and senses.

## *Appendix Two / The Research Effects of Visio Divina on Changing Views of Spirituality*

Eight women and two men — six Anglo-Americans, three African Americans, and one Jamaican — participated in a preliminary study evaluating the effect of Visio Divina in a controlled environment.

### *Procedure*

Visio Divina sessions included ten to fifteen minutes of talking about a previous prayer experience or an issue voiced as a prayer focus, twenty-five to thirty minutes

Visio Divina, and ten to fifteen minutes talking about the experience.

Each person was interviewed and audio taped following the fifteen weekly one-hour Visio Divina sessions. The interview occurred within two weeks following the fifteenth session. The interviewer followed a guide of research questions relating to the themes of faith, hope, and love.

### *Results*

Visio Divina had a positive effect on faith, hope, and love, specifically: Ten of ten showed positive changes in their view of God (faith). Ten of ten showed positive changes in their feeling loved. Nine of ten showed positive changes in how they loved others. Eight of ten showed positive changes in their experience of hope.

### *Changing Views of God*

All ten people reported significant changes in their view of God, primarily in the following areas.

*Increased Trust of God.* Five of the ten people used words to describe God as more trustworthy after experiencing Visio Divina. An additional two of the ten used the word faithful in describing God. For example, one person said, "I trust a lot more that God is faithful and God is present," while another person said, "There is a deep sense in my heart [after experiencing Visio Divina] that God knows what he is doing. I can trust him." One other person said, "God has shown me that there is nothing to be fearful of: he has it all under control. I just have more peace now."

*Experiential Reality of God.* The experiential reality of God gained through Visio Divina was congruent with the cognitive knowledge about God prior to Visio Divina. Often the experience in Visio Divina enabled the person to know God's love and acceptance at a deeper level. Seven of the ten people said they experienced that God is loving. For example, one person said, "I've always had faith, but I am communing much deeper and broader. How high and how wide is the pure love of God?"

*God Reveals God's Self.* The way God seemed to reveal God's self through Visio Divina affected the way people read scripture. As a result, there was a feedback loop of gaining knowledge. Experience in Visio Divina took people into scripture with a new lens, which deepened their understanding of God.

*God's Accessibility.* God became more accessible. Where God had seemed absent or distant prior to Visio Divina, God became accessible with the person's increasing expectation that God would speak to him or her. For example, one person said, "It [Visio Divina] has broadened the ways that I can experience God. Before experiencing Visio Divina, I was able to talk of and be aware of difficult experiences in life, but I've never been able to experience God in the midst of them like through healing of my memories." Another person said, "The vocabulary that God uses with me has really gotten bigger. I am aware that God will speak to me through images, pictures, symbols, stories, and scripture," while yet another person said, "Before experiencing Visio Divina, God was a little bit distant. Now I feel more drawn on my knees with God, and I really find value in that." Another person communicated since experiencing Visio Divina, "I have a greater expectancy that God is going to interact with me."

*Metaphors Changed.* Metaphors used to describe God's character significantly changed as a result of experiencing Visio Divina. Where God had been described previous to Visio Divina as "a loving dictator standing back pointing the finger," after Visio Divina God was described as "kicked back in an easy chair inviting me to sit on his lap." Another person said, "Before experiencing Visio Divina I think I saw God as present. God was loving yet confusing. After Visio Divina I see God as daddy, embracer, and lover. I have a clearer picture of Jesus as daddy with loving arms, giant-sized loving arms." Another person described God as a parent after her experiences of

Visio Divina. She said, "I've heard his parent voice very strongly. I can't really explain it. It is not audible. It is a presence. I experienced many images in Visio Divina where God enters into my childhood memories and loves me like a daddy. I am much more aware of God's parental love."

*Surprised by God.* Six of ten people reported feeling surprised by God after Visio Divina. Five of six said they were specifically surprised that God could enter a painful memory and that God's presence there would bring healing. For example, one person said, "I had no idea that God could change my memory. That blows my mind!" All six were surprised that God would reveal Jesus as identifying with their emotions in the midst of the memory and would reveal God's reaction to the pain or trauma. One participant said, "I was amazed and even dumbfounded by Jesus' response [in the memory]. He would be crying, hurt, writhing in pain, weeping. It was an awesome thing to know that he cares about me in that way, that he knows the pain I felt."

### Changing Views of Hope

Eight of ten people in the study experienced positive change in their view of the future, primarily in one area. Six of the ten said their view of the future was positive because God would be with them. Their view was not based on what God was going to do: it was based on the reality that God was going to be with them. For example, one person said, "In experiencing God's love, just the way I am, there is a lot of hope, and it's really neat." He also said, "I don't have a plan for the future anymore. God plans the future. I just follow God's path." Another person who struggled with much anxiety over her future career said, "God wants me to cling to him and not cling to the degree, the income, etc. So it is funny because I have hopes for my future, but I still have no clue exactly what it holds. There is hope in the trust [of God]."

### *Learning Self-Love*

Eight of ten people experienced a positive change in their ability to love themselves, primarily in three areas.

*Increased Self-Acceptance.* As most people experienced God accepting them during Visio Divina, their acceptance of themselves increased. One person said, "I am imperfect and everybody else is imperfect, but God is going to still love us. We're called to love each other, so here we go." Another person said, "I am able to embrace myself more. I am learning how to love myself and accept that I am lovable." Yet another said, "I definitely see progress in self-acceptance, but I have a long way to go."

Yet another said, "What has been very freeing is to know that God's acceptance of me takes the pressure off being driven and having to achieve goals."

*Increased Self-Esteem.* Most people said they liked themselves more and began to be able to love themselves in practical ways that were different. For example, one person said she is better able to take care of herself. Another said she is able to confront others in ways she had not been able to before Visio Divina. Yet another said she is able to speak up in the moment to defend her self. Yet another said, "I see myself as more capable and stronger because of this whole process." The same person said, "I see my own needs as important as the needs of others." This was a significant change in the way she viewed herself as she came for Visio Divina as a result of being in a physically abusive marriage where she continually deferred her needs to the needs of her husband. Another person said, "God is changing my identity by giving me some beautiful pictures of him being my community. My sense of self is coming from God. I like what I am seeing in myself."

*Increased Self-Knowledge.* All ten people said they knew themselves better after Visio Divina. Their words communicated they better understood how past experiences shaped their behaviors and thoughts. They said they understood their current behaviors in light of their past painful experiences and subsequently responded to those behaviors with such insight. One person said, "I feel like I've experienced healing and I have more insight into what needed to be healed." Another said, "I am more aware of where things come from within me." While yet another said, "I can care for myself now because I have more self knowledge. I am finding out ways that I used to escape. Now I can see the pattern and say, 'Oh, I am escaping right now.'" One other person said, "I still get anxious, but now I know what is going on. I notice it before I react to it."

### *Learning to Love Others*

Nine of ten people experienced a positive change in how they loved others, primarily in two areas.

*Increased Acceptance of Others.* Most people said that in experiencing God's accepting them during Visio Divina, they were more accepting of others. One person said, "I am more gracious to myself: I see that I am more gracious to others." Another person said, "I sense God more completely as one who so wholeheartedly embraces and accepts me. Then I think likewise seeing God wholeheartedly accepting and embracing others." Yet another said, "Visio Divina has forced me to look at myself and say, 'How am I not accepting? How am I not tolerant of others? The way God has accepted me in Visio Divina is the way I am supposed to accept others.' "

*Others Recognized How They Changed.* Significant others noticed a positive change in people. Family members and friends verbally noticed that they seemed to live differently as a result of Visio Divina. One person who was struggling with uncontrollable anger and rage prior to Visio Divina said, "I am sure people feel much safer around me." Another person, whose mother is a social worker and was very cautious and concerned about her daughter participating in this study, said her mother wanted to refer someone to the primary researcher for spiritual direction and Visio Divina. One other person said, "My relationship with my parents has changed a lot. I am able to give them more freedom to be who they are and not expect them to love me in a way only God can. I am letting them be free." The same person also said, "I am more fully known by my parents and they still love me. Wow! That has been really good."

One person did not know if others saw a difference in her. She did not communicate that she viewed others differently. She said that she had not thought about it. She was struggling with implications of having physical disabilities that severely impacted her understanding of how others viewed her. She communicated difficulty in experiencing God's acceptance and love in past painful memories because "it doesn't change anything." She said that the past experiences were real, and just seeing Jesus with her in the pain did not change the fact that God had not healed her of her physical limitations. This person initially had difficulty experiencing God through Visio Divina because of her disappointment with God for his not healing her physical body after many years of asking him to do so.

## *Appendix Three / Charisms of Grace / Spiritual Gifts*

The following discussion on charisms of grace/spiritual gifts is taken from the book *Spiritual Gifts*, written by Dr. Robert J. Clinton. The term "charism of grace" can be substituted each time "spiritual gift" is used.

The study of spiritual gifts can be controversial. It is important to avoid two extremes: first, neglect of the whole subject because of problems and disagreements, and, second, overemphasis on spiritual gifts as a cure-all for the church. Listed below are some problems as well as principles to help avoid both extremes.

## *Problems*

1. Disagreement: There is disagreement as to the definitions of the gifts of and even the existence of certain gifts.

2. Neglect: There is ignorance and even neglect of spiritual gifts in many churches.

3. Confusion between supernatural and natural: There is confusion concerning the relationship between spiritual gifts and natural abilities.

4. Abuses of gifts: Certain spiritual gifts are emphasized by some as signs of a necessary work of the Holy Spirit. This emphasis at best causes spiritual pride, and at worst can be divisive.

## *Principles*

1. Disagreements usually indicate the lack of conclusive biblical evidence upon which to resolve the questions. Tolerance of other views is necessary.

2. Be aware of stressing one gift above another.

3. Make sure you know the difference between fruit of the Spirit and gifts of the Spirit. Paul describes the fruit of the Spirit as "love, joy, peace, patience, kindness, generosity, faithfulness, gentleness, and

self-control" (Galatians 5:22–23). Fruit indicates spiritual maturity. Gifts are for service.

The scriptural ideal seems to be the exercise of the gifts of the Spirit and the expression of the fruit of the Spirit concurrently. Both gifts and fruit are signs of the Spirit in a life.

Maturity is primarily indicated by manifesting the fruit of the Spirit, not by the presence of gifts or even their powerful exercise.

## *Definitions of Spiritual Gifts*

**Prophecy:** The gift of prophecy is the capacity to express truth (of a predictive nature as well as explanatory) from God in order to exhort, edify, or console.

**Word of Wisdom:** The gift of word of wisdom represents the capacity to know the mind of the Spirit in a given situation and to communicate clearly the situation, facts, truth, or application of facts and truth to meet the need of the situation.

**Word of Knowledge:** The gift of word of knowledge represents the capacity to receive supernaturally revealed knowledge which otherwise could not or would not be known. It has been the experience of people and groups which recognize this gift used in conjunction with the revealing of knowledge concerning healing.

**Faith:** The gift of faith is that unusual capacity to recognize in a given situation that which God intends to do perhaps generally or specifically and to trust God for it until is comes to pass. It is most likely expressed through prayer with God (that is, the prayer of faith), though it may simply be a belief in a vision of what God can and will do in some situation.

**Healing:** The gifts of healing refer to the supernatural ability to heal people in response to a laying on of hands or praying for healing by the person having the gift.

**Mercy:** The gift of mercy refers to the capacity both to feel sympathy with those in need (especially those suffering) and to manifest this sympathy in some practical helpful way so as to encourage and help those in need.

**Discernment of Spirits:**[1] The gift of discerning of spirits refers to the special ability that God gives to some members of the body of Christ to know whether certain behavior is influenced by the Holy Spirit or the demonic.

---

1. This definition does not come from Dr. Robert J. Clinton's book *Spiritual Gifts*. The definition is my synthesis from various writers who discuss the topic of spiritual gifts/charisms of grace.

# References

Adam, A.K.M., editor

  2000   *Handbook of Postmodern Biblical Interpretation.* St. Louis:
         Chalice Press.

Aichele, George, et al.

  1995   *The Postmodern Bible: The Bible and Culture Collective.*
         New Haven, CT: Yale University Press.

Ainsworth, Mary

  1969   "Object Relations, Dependency and Attachment: A
         Theoretical Review of the Infant-Mother Relationship."
         *Child Development,* 40:969–1025.

  1985   "Patterns of Infant-Mother Attachments: Antecedents
         and Effects on Development." *Bulletin of the New York
         Academy of Medicine,* 61:771–91.

Bowlby, John

  1988   *A Secure Base: Parent-Child Attachment and Healthy Human
         Development.* 2nd ed. New York: Basic Books.

Clinton, Robert J.

  1985   *Spiritual Gifts.* Beaverlodge, Alberta, Canada: Horizon
         House Publishers.

Clinton, Tim, and Gary Sibcy

    2002    *Attachments: Why You Love, Feel, and Act the Way You Do.*
               Brentwood, TN: Integrity Publishers.

Craigie, Peter C.

    1983    *Psalms 1–50.* Word Biblical Commentary 19. Waco,
               TX: Word Books.

Fitzmyer, Joseph A.

    1993    *Romans: A New Translation with Introduction and
               Commentary.* Anchor Bible 33. New York: Doubleday.

Huber, Karen

    2003    "Life after Childhood Divorce." Accessed July 15,
               2003. *www.relevantmagazine.com/modules.php?op=
               modload&name=News&file=article&sid=151.*

Lee, Dorothy A.

    1994    *The Symbolic Narratives of the Fourth Gospel: The Interplay
               of Form and Meaning.* Sheffield, England: JSOT Press.

Lewis, H. B.

    1980    " 'Narcissistic Personality' or 'Shame-Prone Superego
               Mode.' " *Comprehensive Psychotherapy* 1:59–80.

Mahedy, William, and Janet Bernardi

    1994    *A Generation Alone: Xers Making a Place in the World.*
               Downers Grove, IL: InterVarsity Press.

May, Gerald G.

    1982    *Will and Spirit: A Contemplative Psychology.* San Francisco:
               HarperSanFrancisco.

1988    *Addiction and Grace.* San Francisco: HarperSan-
        Francisco.

1991    *The Awakened Heart: Living Beyond Addiction.* San
        Francisco: HarperSanFrancisco.

Mitchell, David C.

1997    *The Message of the Psalter: An Eschatological Programme in
        the Book of Psalms.* Sheffield, UK: Sheffield Academic
        Press.

Sanford, John A.

1993    *Mystical Christianity: A Psychological Commentary on the
        Gospel of John.* New York: Crossroad.

Schneiders, Sandra

1991    *The Revelatory Text: Interpreting the New Testament as
        Sacred Scripture.* San Francisco: HarperSanFrancisco.

2000    "Scripture and Spirituality." In *Christian Spiritual-
        ity: Origins to the Twelfth Century,* ed. B. McGinn,
        J. Meyendorf, and J. Leclercq, 1–19. New York:
        Crossroad.

Schore, Allan N.

2003a   *Affect Dysregulation and Disorders of the Self.* New York:
        W. W. Norton.

2003b   *Affect Regulation and the Repair of the Self.* New York:
        W. W. Norton.

Schottroff, Luise

1995    *Lydia's Impatient Sisters: A Feminist Social History of
        Early Christianity.* Louisville: Westminster John Knox
        Press.

Schüssler Fiorenza, Elisabeth

    1994    *Jesus: Miriam's Child, Sophia's Prophet: Critical Issues in Feminist Christology.* New York: Crossroad.

Siegel, Daniel J.

    1999    *The Developing Mind: How Relationships and the Brain Interact to Shape Who We Are.* New York: Guilford Press.

Weiser, Artur

    1962    *The Psalms.* Philadelphia: Westminster.

Wenham, Gordon J.

    1987    *Genesis 1–15.* Word Biblical Commentary 1. Waco, TX: Word Books.

Winnicott, D. W.

    1958    "The Capacity to Be Alone." *International Journal of Psychoanalysis* 39:416–20.

Wray, Judith Hoch

    1998    *Rest as a Theological Metaphor in the Epistle to the Hebrews and the Gospel of Truth: Early Christian Homiletics of Rest.* SBL Dissertation Series 166. Atlanta: Scholars Press.

# Acknowledgments

Relationships are central to any project having meaning and value. There are many people whose presence in my life contributed to finishing this book. Without these friends, this book would have been much less enjoyable to write and not nearly as insightful. Ten GenXers and their experiences of Visio Divina made the project possible. I appreciate your willingness to allow me to journey with you into deep places within your soul. My life is more meaningful because of your openness to God and our shared experiences. Living our stories, passions, struggles, and gifts in a women's group called the "Diamonds" also created a space for ideas to emerge while motivating me to write when I felt discouraged. Thank you, Alison, Deborah, Jane, Kristiana, Megan, and Suzanne.

Friendships that remain close beyond a few years are rare. I am especially grateful for my friend Susan Mull, who provided support and insight that broadened and deepened my understanding of how the soul is transformed. Jane Thomson offered endless encouragement while advocating for justice thousands of miles away in Iraq, Sudan, and Afghanistan. Many other people during the past few years inspired me and helped this book come into existence. Thank you to Carmen Renee Berry, Rosanne Janzti, Jan Zeisman, Tom Adams, Alan Fadling, Margie Waldo, Karen Nelson, Andrew Thomson, and the community of the Pecos Benedictine Monastery.

A wise editor is essential for a book with new ideas to come to print. Roy M. Carlisle, senior editor at The Crossroad Publishing Company, provided such wisdom and the expertise I needed to believe that people would want to read about and experience Visio Divina.

My dissertation committee also supported and encouraged my writing this book. "Empowering of women" and "courageous" are words that describe my experience of my PhD mentor, Wilbert Shenk. "Wise" and "patient" are words that describe my experience of postmodern Old Testament scholar John Goldingay, and "spiritual depth" and "perseverance" are words that describe my experience of psychologist Janice Strength. Each of these brilliant scholars inspired and invited me to apply my mind more rigorously, but it is their personhood that impacted me the most.

Creative and artistic communicators don't usually get much done without a talented person behind the scenes paying attention to details and helping clarify the message. Thank you to copyeditor RH for your invaluable feedback.

Sometimes words cannot contain the emotion or express the depth of meaning and appreciation to Love. In the silence it is known. Amen.

# About the Author

Life is most meaningful for Karen when she feels connected with God, herself, and others. During this season of her life, connection with God is nurtured through contemplative prayer and identifying with God the potter while practicing the art of ceramics. Connection with herself is nurtured through dialog with a spiritual director, paying attention to her soul by learning from her dreams, and taking walks in the mountains with "Romi," an Australian shepherd pup. Connection with others is nurtured through friendships, soul mates, a woman's group and family, belonging in the Pecos Benedictine community, and trying to love and be present with her directees while working as a spiritual director in private practice in Pasadena, California. She especially enjoys working with women who have been marginalized by society, the church and/or their families.

Karen received a certificate in spiritual direction from the Pecos Benedictine Monastery in Pecos, New Mexico, and holds an MA in Theology and a PhD from Fuller Theological Seminary and an MA in Counseling from Northern Arizona University. Her dissertation focused on spirituality and transformation among postmoderns. She has been an adjunct instructor at Fuller while also teaching various seminars on spiritual formation and healing. Karen lives in Southern California.

# A Word from the Editor

Karen and I must affirm the power of the network! We first met at one of my writing workshops where I teach writers about the Myers-Briggs Type Indicator and its use in understanding the strengths and weaknesses of particular writing styles. Our host and workshop co-ordinator, Carmen Renee Berry, thoughtfully seated us across from each other at lunch so we could talk about what Karen was working on in her Ph.D. program and the book that might emerge out of that. That was four years ago.

So Karen and I now have this wonderful history of networking over a period of years and in myriad places. We met in restaurants and at conferences all over the country to make sure we kept in touch about the project. We have been in Toronto, LA, Anaheim, Pasadena, Glendale, New York, Chicago, and various other places. I was determined to make sure we met so that she would know that my support for this book was tenacious and that I would do whatever I could do to support her through the process of making it happen. And she labored through her Ph.D. dissertation, her Spiritual Direction training, and setting up her new ministry at the same time that she was slowly working away at the writing of the book. She has the work ethic of someone who has a vision of her own strengths and gifts and is willing to go the extra mile to make sure her work in the world is established and helping others.

All through this process Karen would always humbly inquire about what she had to do next to make her manuscript ready for publication. I distinctly remember one meeting on a cool, clear morning in southern California. After several minutes of looking for an open restaurant, we finally found one that had seating at an outside table. We had come together to review the newest version of the manuscript. I had some tough things to say about what she had to do to the manuscript and she didn't blink an eye. She acknowledged the work that was needed, and said she would get to it.

There are always moments like that in the editorial process of developing a project where you know that the author really has the courage and skill to do what has to be done. Richard Foster once remarked to me that he thought "the mark of personal maturity is knowing what has to be done and doing it." Karen is one of those people who figures out what needs to be done, obtains relevant guidance, and then does it. It takes a clear heart to do that in the world. Many of us flinch on seeing that something tough must be done, knowing that it will be hard and wishing we really didn't have to work that hard or be that honest.

This is the kind of book that looks you straight in the eye and says, "This is going to be hard, but I am here to walk with you on this difficult journey, and we will find healing together." A book that does that is worth reading. A book that looks you straight in the eye and risks the challenge of growth with you is worth more than just reading; it is worth really diving into and taking the risk of opening your heart to. This is one of those books. You have my word on that.

*Roy M. Carlisle*
*Senior Editor*

*Of Related Interest*

**Carmen Renee Berry**
**WHEN HELPING YOU IS HURTING ME**
*Escaping the Messiah Trap*

Carmen Renee Berry, best known as the co-author of the million-selling *girlfriends*, first appeared on the national scene with the publishing phenomenon that started everyone talking about the Messiah Trap and how to overcome it. With her unsurpassed ability as a writer and teacher, Berry shows how we can help others only once we learn to love ourselves.

"Messiahs try to be helpful wherever they go. Wherever Messiahs can be found, you can be sure they will be busy taking care of other people. Do you find yourself trapped in a relationship where you do all the giving and the other person does all the taking?" If so, you have fallen into the Messiah Trap. This book is your ticket out.

0-8245-2108-0, $16.95 paperback

crossroad

*Of Related Interest*

**Lyn Doucet and Robin Hebert**
**WHEN WOMEN PRAY**
*Our Personal Stories of Extraordinary Grace*

"We are two ordinary women who, through God's
grace, have had extraordinary experiences of prayer.
In this book we share several of these experiences.
We have no final answers about God, for in prayer we
have experienced God as a beautiful dance of mystery.
And yet . . . we know that in the presence of this dance
of love we have been transformed. And we now desire
to invite you into this sacred dance of daily commu-
nion with God." Includes original prayers and helpful
tips for praying.

ISBN 0-8245-2279-6, $16.95 paperback

crossroad

*Of Related Interest*

**Birell Walsh**
**PRAYING FOR OTHERS**
*Powerful Practices for Healing, Peace,*
*and New Beginnings*

In the tradition of Larry Dossey's *Prayer Is Good Medicine* comes this healing, holistic book on a topic little covered on bookshelves or in the media. *Praying for Others* weaves together prayer success stories from a variety of faith traditions, including Zen, Cabala, Sufism, and Christianity, along with Walsh's own journey toward wholeness through prayer.

0-8245-1949-3, $16.95 paperback

Please support your local bookstore,
or call 1-800-707-0670 for Customer Service.

For a free catalog, write us at

THE CROSSROAD PUBLISHING COMPANY
16 Penn Plaza – 481 Eighth Avenue, Suite 1550
New York, NY 10001

Visit our website at
*www.cpcbooks.com*
All prices subject to change.

crossroad